MW00876357

Ingrid Bergman

An Ingrid Bergman Biography

Katy Holborn

Copyright © 2017.

All rights reserved. No part of this publication may be reproduced, distributed, or transmitted in any form or by any means, including photocopying, recording, or other electronic or mechanical methods, without the prior written permission of the publisher, except in the case of brief quotations embodied in critical reviews and certain other noncommercial uses permitted by copyright law.

This book is intended for informational and entertainment purposes only. The publisher limits all liability arising from this work to the fullest extent of the law.

Table of Contents

Ingrid Bergman – The Actress and the Woman

Introduction

Hollywood's Golden Age cameramen, upon whose lenses crossed some of the world's greatest beauties, were theoretically a jaded bunch who had seen it all. But Swedish star Ingrid Bergman, a magnetic actress of natural incandescence, commanded their attention.

They called her beauty "bulletproof."

Ingrid Bergman - with her intelligent and expressive blue eyes, full lips, high cheekbones and a broad, noble forehead - could be shot from any angle. The cameramen were not the only ones called to rapt attention by the stunning actress. Critics and audiences alike (not to mention her directors and co-stars) found her irresistible. Beyond beautiful, she was compelling; able to command a room and show courage, yet also convey compassion and vulnerability.

Her approach to work, like her looks and acting style, was a breath of fresh air in a town of inflated egos, too. She had discipline and an even temperament such that on set, she was straightforward and always prepared. Off-screen she was unaffected and unpretentious, strolling around in little make-up and low heels, ready with an easy smile or a big laugh. She was a pragmatic, down-to-earth woman, who could eat several ice creams in a day, and found designer clothes expensive. She was even an outfit repeater to the Academy Awards.

She was a gifted and versatile actress, as adventurous in life as she was with art. She wanted to explore her craft and spread her wings, but by her features, mannerisms and some of her most memorable roles in the 1940s, she had a morally-upright, almost saintly image in the industry. Not that she actively cultivated it herself; everyone, she had once been quoted as saying, *"has shades of bad and good."*

The weight of that saintly image and the lofty expectations it inspired, may have been the reason for the public's extremely poor reception of her infamous love affair with Italian neorealist director, Roberto Rossellini. The scandal would permanently change the trajectory of her previously unblemished career. She had fallen in love with a man she greatly admired and they began an affair.

She became pregnant before her divorce was finalized. It was 1949 and the codes of morality were dramatically less malleable than they seem now, or even just a few years later at the rise of the sexual revolution in the 1960s. In the meantime, change needed a martyr and Bergman made for a convenient, prominent blood sacrifice.

The nation's conservative element was in a panic-mongering uproar. She'd been called an agent of evil, and as one United States senator boldly claimed, *"a better Hollywood"* would come *"out of Ingrid Bergman's ashes."*

The scandal would see her public image ripped apart, from the tabloids and newspapers to religious groups and the halls of Washington. Studios were discouraged from hiring her. Her actions were condemned at the U.S. Senate. People boycotted her films. She fled to Europe amidst the upheaval. At what could have been the height of her beauty and talent – she was only 34 years old and an Oscar award-winning actress - she wouldn't be seen again in American screens until seven years later. Even with a triumphant return (marked by another Oscar, no less!), most of her movie work after the scandal would still be filmed in Europe.

A Hollywood Heavyweight

Ingrid Bergman holds pride of place as one of Hollywood's greatest actresses. Her Academy Award wins tie with our generation's own, beloved Meryl Streep, and they are both second only to four-time winner, Golden Age great, Katherine Hepburn.

Ingrid Bergman's Oscars came at very important points of her life.

In 1945, she was honored with the statuette for Best Actress in a Leading Role for her work in *Gaslight* (1944). It was her first win but her second nomination, following the previous year's *For Whom the Bell Tolls* (1943), and was a firm stamp of approval from her new home in Hollywood. Her peers were effusive with admiration for Ingrid Bergman at this high point of her career. Academy Award-winning actress, Jennifer Jones, handed her the important award with even more meaningful words; Bergman's artistry, she had said, "*won our vote.*" But it was her graciousness that "*won our hearts.*" One of Bergman's fellow-nominees that year, Barbara Stanwyck, was just as generous with praise. She had called the victorious Ingrid

Bergman her favorite actress, and counted herself amongst *the Ingrid Bergman Fan Club.*"

Her second Oscar was for *Anastasia* (1956). The film came about seven years after Hollywood and America's self-proclaimed arbiters of morality condemned her for her relationship with Roberto Rossellini and crafted her dramatic downfall in 1949. If that was not enough discouragement from hiring the disgraced actress for the extremely coveted lead role, her last American film was all the way back in 1948 for Victor Fleming's *Joan of Arc* – and that did not at all do well in the box office. But the Ukrainian-born director tapped to helm the project, Anatole Litvak, and studio head, Daryl F. Zanuck, were convinced Ingrid Bergman was the right actress to bring *Anastasia* to life. They were right to bat for her before the powers-that-be over at 20th Century Fox. Critics and audiences loved her performance and she would win her second Academy Award for Best Actress in a Leading Role. That Ingrid Bergman was great in the movie shouldn't have come as a surprise, however – she is good in any movie to begin with, but *Anastasia* was the story of a woman in exile making her way back… just like Ingrid Bergman herself. With a hit film and an Oscar in hand, the unstoppable Swede was back, and for good.

Ingrid Bergman's final Oscar, as Best Actress in the Supporting Role category, was for Sidney Lumet's star-studded film adaptation of Agatha Christie's *Murder on the Orient Express* (1974). It was, in the words of co-star Lauren Bacall, *"a blinding cast -"* for how else could anyone describe a movie that included Bergman, Bacall, Albert Finney, Sean Connery, Vanessa Redgrave, Anthony Perkins, Martin Balsam and Jacqueline Bisset? Around the time she was cast with such heavyweights, however, Bergman was diagnosed with breast cancer. She would suffer from the ailment for almost a decade, before it claimed her life, on her birthday, in 1982. She was 67 years old.

Made for the Movies

Ingrid Bergman's life is shaped like a classic narrative structure. She had once said she wanted the public to take her as an actress separate from her identity as a woman, but even in real life, it's as if she was made for the movies.

At the beginning there was her childhood years, marred by character-building tragedies. The rising action followed her ascent up the Hollywood ladder, marking both professional successes and a building tension as her creative energies sought and found Roberto Rossellini, just as her woman's heart did. Together, they sailed into scandal that would herald the fight for a comeback. At the climax of the story is *Anastasia*, and the question of whether her return would be phoenix-like and decisive in its triumph. The falling action followed the rest of her work and the decline in her health, until she made her quiet exit, passing right on her birthday.

What she left behind was a body of work that few in her profession could match in quality. Her performances throughout were all at once intelligent, gutsy and touching, but her approach to her cinematic life's vicissitudes was just as worthy of attention and admiration.

She followed her art. She followed her heart. She treated other people with respect and lived her life, even with the mammoth scandal that would come to define a large part of it, with dignity. She was a consummate professional and a caring mother. She was a passionate performer who had courage and integrity. She met her cancer head on and pushed herself through pain and difficulty. She looked at everyday she lived and worked beyond it as a victory. Ingrid Bergman is made immortal by all of these.

Other Areas of Development

Stockholm syndrome isn't just limited to developing in hostages or victims of kidnappings. It can also be found in a wider variety of circumstances.

In any situation where two opposing parties are reduced to the status of victim and offender, it is possible for Stockholm syndrome to manifest. For example, many abused children or victims of domestic violence will voluntarily stay with their abusers, despite having the freedom to leave should they wish. However, because they have come to associate abuse with their prolonged survival, they deem that leaving the situation will leave them worse off. Similarly, sex workers who are regularly punished by their procurers (colloquially:

pimps or madams) may also come to develop deep affections for those who abuse them because, in many ways, their procurers are responsible for their survival.

Stockholm syndrome is also common amongst cult members. Because, in the case of many cults, a person has willingly given over their livelihood to a leader or group of leaders, they are already consciously aware that many aspects of their survival are in the hands of someone else. This is a kind of 'voluntary' Stockholm syndrome which people enter into, therefore bypassing the trauma which comes with being taken hostage. Therefore, transitioning into the later stages of the condition happens easier and with less resistance. A similar type of relationship can be seen in sadomasochistic,

BDSM-based relationships between a dominant partner and a submissive partner.

The application of Stockholm syndrome has proven to be beneficial in regards to ensuring the survival of the hostage in question. To the captor, the symptoms which accompany Stockholm syndrome developing in the hostage may interfere with the captor's ability to carry out their intended plans accordingly. If a hostage is displaying affection towards them, it may be difficult for the captor to kill their hostage or harm them to the severity which they originally intended.

Stockholm syndrome has come to be known as many different things over the past few decades since it become a recognized phenomenon; Helsinki syndrome, traumatic bonding, Uncle Tom syndrome, plus other colloquial terms. At their core, all these conditions come down to the same kind of reaction: survival techniques employed by those who still possess the desire to live, despite the horrific circumstances they may find themselves subjected to.

Early Life

Frieda Henrietta Adler and Justus Samuel Bergman had their daughter and only child, Ingrid, on the 29th of August, 1915 in Stockholm Sweden. Frieda was German and Justus, Swedish. The couple had lost two children early before Ingrid came along, and she would have no siblings to follow her. As a youngster, she was said to have coped by crafting imaginary friends; a gift for imagination and pretend that would herald her acting abilities. But her life became lonelier in far more tragic ways.

Frieda passed away when Ingrid was around two years old, leaving behind Justus and their daughter. By many accounts, Justus was a doting father. He owned a camera shop and enjoyed taking pictures of his lovely little girl who eventually became a natural in front of the camera. Unfortunately, he too would pass a decade after his wife. Justus succumbed to stomach cancer when Ingrid was just 12. At so tender an age, Ingrid Bergman was already an orphan. She reportedly came to live with an aunt, whom she would also lose shortly afterwards at age 13. She eventually came under the care of an elderly uncle and his family.

The time she spent before her father's camera and how he cultivated her creativity is unsurprisingly credited for Ingrid Bergman having performance on her mind from an early age. She attended private school and participated in plays. In her diaries (and she wrote of her life extensively), she had mentioned being the head of the theater club in school.

Eventually, she landed her first job in film. She was only 15 when she appeared as an extra for a Swedish studio. In *Landskamp* (1932) she was uncredited, just a girl waiting in a line of many other girls. But the experience would only encourage further pursuit of the arts; she compared the studio to hallowed ground.

After high school, she secured a scholarship and enrolled at the Royal Dramatic Theater, but she wouldn't stay for very long. She wanted very much to be a part of the thriving Swedish cinema, which had already launched the great Greta Garbo into Hollywood greatness. She was very determined and by some accounts, had asked her uncle, a florist, to help her get an audition by connecting her with one of his customers, the actor / director / talent coordinator, Karin Swanstrom. Other accounts credit a friend of her late father's for the link to Swanstrom. Either way, Swanstrom gave her a shot, and thereafter reportedly made arrangements for Ingrid to test with director, Gustaf Molander. Molander did not give her the big break (though they would work well in Swedish films, later), but her talent and tenacity would eventually find her working in the industry anyway.

Talent and tenacity indeed, Ingrid Bergman had in spades. But other accounts of her rise to stardom suggest a far less wholesome origin story for the Hollywood legend. She may have been romantically involved with the actor and director, Edvin Adolphson... even while she was in a relationship with Peter Lindstrom, whom she would eventually marry. It has been alleged that Ingrid Bergman's first speaking role, for *Munkbrogreven* ("*The Count of the Old Town* ") (1935), was due to Adolphson giving his girl an expanded part and made himself her screen partner.

However way she may have gotten her foot in the door for a breakthrough role, Ingrid Bergman gave it her best shot. *Munkbrogreven* was a romantic comedy, but her scenes proved she could act with subtlety and convey complexity. Here she plays Elsa, a chambermaid working in a hotel in Stockholm's Old Town. The cast of characters includes crooks, policemen, aristocrats and other colorful eccentrics, all mired in the mystery surrounding the town's elusive jewel thief. Her performance was well-received, earning critical praise. But she would also be criticized for her figure, which ran to tall and hefty. It wouldn't be enough to hinder her quick ascent.

When she left the Royal Dramatic Theater to pursue a professional career, she had reportedly frustrated its director, Olaf Molander, who had feared for her raw talent if she plunged straight into movie work without enough technique. But she knew what she wanted and she had confidence in herself. Sure enough, by the age of 19, she landed a deal with Swedish Films. She was not paid much, but she reportedly got to keep her movie wardrobe, they reportedly funded her drama lessons, and she had ample opportunities for work. Soon, she was a real working actress and eventually, a star.

Intermezzo (1936) is the movie that would change her life forever. The film was directed and co-written by Gustaf Molander, who is said to have crafted it with her in mind. As Anita Hoffman, she is the radiant, young piano teacher who has a May-December romance with her student's still-married father, a world-famous concern violinist. The movie, and Bergman in it, bowled over critics in Sweden, but also in other countries.

She became more able to select challenging roles. She bravely took on the part of a disfigured criminal embittered and made vicious by a tragic childhood fire, who finds beauty and noble purpose again in *En Kvinnas Ansikte* ("*A Woman's Face*") (1938). But Bergman was a bit of a restless artist at the time and she wanted more. The local scene became too small for her. She wanted to spread her wings, and her desire unfortunately blew her into late-1930s Germany.

She signed with the German studio UFA, but realized to her regret that Nazi party membership was prominent in key persons of the entertainment industry. She made the feminist romantic comedy, *Die vier Gesellen* (*"The Four Companions"*) (1938) with UFA but soon fled back to Sweden.

As her German misadventure was unfolding, *Intermezzo* was taking an interesting tour around the hallowed halls of the entertainment world across the Atlantic. If the stories are true – and fact could sometimes be stranger than fiction, especially when it comes to Hollywood - the movie was beloved by two Swedish immigrants whose son, worked as elevator operator at a Park Avenue address in New

York. That Park Avenue apartment was home to Kay Brown, who had been assigned by legendary producer, David O. Selznick, to find European movies to remake for the American market. The elevator operator reportedly gave Brown the hot tip, and Brown was bowled over by Ingrid Bergman's performance and radiance. Selznick, on the other hand, delighted in the movie right away, but not necessarily its lead actress. He worried that Bergman's name was too German at a time when it was an inconvenient association. He worried about her English skills. He even worried about her eyebrows!

Eventually though, Selznick changed his mind and sent Brown off on a mission to secure not only the rights to make an American version of the film, but also to acquire the talents of its young Swedish star. Bergman, who has fielded Hollywood offers before, played it cool. She had always wanted to be an international actress, but under the right conditions. She had also just given birth to her and husband Dr. Peter Lindstrom's first child, Pia.

Bergman did not want the standard, seven-year contract and desired only to commit to one film. She reportedly needed to have a better feel first of whether or not she wanted to remain in Hollywood. She got what she asked for, and was soon on her way to the United States. It wouldn't be the last time she pushed her will into the system.

When she arrived in Hollywood, plans were initially made to subject her to a dramatic makeover – changes were intended for her teeth, her hair, hey eyebrows and even her

German-sounding name. What they couldn't change (but also fretted about of course) was her height; she was 5'9".

Not that she allowed them to significantly alter anything about her anyway. They must have seen something in her when they brought her in, she reasoned, so why the need for change? She did, however, do well in personal voice coaching to ease her heavy accent. Little else would change – she even disliked heavy makeup. Selznick, who had a nose for opportunity, reportedly made lemonades out of his new acquisition's "lemons." She was sold for her naturalness; a rarity in Hollywood at the time.

That word – "natural" – would trail her throughout her career, in reference to her fresh features, her unaffected manner and her seemingly effortless screen presence.

Natural...

There was a new breed of Hollywood actress on the scene, and she was going to take the town by storm.

The Actress

Of acting, Ingrid Bergman once said that you do it *"because you must."* That compulsion to perform before the camera has pushed her since childhood, from the time she spent before her doting father's lenses, to the performances she did in school, the education she pursued, the Swedish film industry she conquered, and the Hollywood scene she invaded. It was her sense of artistry that helped her pick projects. It is what brought her into the path of her great romance - and her great downfall. But it was also what helped her find redemption and career resurrection.

In acting there was refuge from a painful childhood. When she got older, in acting there was freedom from the pain of cancer.

And after she passed away - in acting, film was forever and so was Ingrid Bergman.

From 1932 to 1982 – a fifty year career – she has 55 film credits and dozens of nominations and awards, the most notable being two Academy Awards in the Leading Actress category and one in the Supporting category. She has honors from the Golden Globes and BAFTAs, too. But she was also found on the small screen (with Primetime Emmys to honor her), as well as on the stage (with a Tony). Her feats have made her amongst the most decorated actors in Hollywood. She was clearly compelling anywhere she went, on any medium she would grace. But some of her performances stand out over others. Aside from *Intermezzo* mentioned above, here are a few of the most important and most memorable performances of "Bulletproof" Ingrid Bergman:

- **Her First Oscar Nomination**. Ingrid Bergman was already beloved in Hollywood by the time she won for *Gaslight* at the age of 30. It wasn't even her first nomination; that distinction goes to *For Whom the Bell Tolls* (1943). Ernest Hemingway's 1940 hit novel was adapted for the screen by Paramount, with his friend, Gary Cooper, in the lead. In her usual assertive fashion, Ingrid Bergman made a play for the leading lady, and had impressed Hemingway himself. For a miscellany of reasons, however, the role went to Vera Zorina instead. It was soon clear that the actress picked over

Bergman was not working out, however, and Bergman was eventually called in for the rescue just as *Casablanca* was wrapping.

For Whom the Bell Tolls is set in the Spanish Civil War and follows the story of Robert Jordan (Gary Cooper), an American volunteer who joins a group of guerillas fighting the fascists. While on a mission to destroy a critical bridge, he falls for Maria (Ingrid Bergman), a female guerilla member who had been abused by a fascist faction. She was damaged and brutalized, but still remained pure. The dynamiter's mission is complicated by his changed feelings about life stemming from his love of Maria, but also by complex, lethal guerilla politics.

The film adaptation shied away from Hemingway's politics, but it hyped up the romantic elements of the story to good cinematic effect, and the movie was well-received. It also may have helped that Ingrid Bergman had felt a real, if ultimately platonic, attraction to her fetching leading man.

- **Casablanca (1942).** *Casablanca* is an indelible film in cinema history, beloved across generations. A true Golden Age output, it was Hollywood classic *par excellence,* but with singular wit, cool factor and a light edge. It is treasured by the industry... though this was reportedly not quite the case for its female star!

Casablanca in Morocco is home to the nightclub, "Rick's Café Americain," early in World War II. The hot property is the hangout of choice for expats, refugees, crooks, gamblers and officials. Its proprietor is Humphrey Bogart's embittered Rick, a world-weary cynic who finds himself in the role of reluctant hero when his old flame, Ingrid Bergman's luminous Ilsa, and Ilsa's husband, a resistance fighter on the run, walk into his life in need of help.

Casablanca is a beautiful story, beautifully told on the screen, and is essential viewing not only for fans of Ingrid Bergman, but for all lovers of film. It has stood the test of time – though the leading lady was reportedly somewhat dissatisfied with it. As a serious actress who wanted to fully understand and inhabit her character, she may have been thrown off by the unconventional way it was written and shot. There were half a dozen writers re-writing the script all the time, it was said, which reportedly frustrated Bergman as she did not know where her character was headed. She was, however, still undeniably lovely in it.

- *Gaslight* **(1944).** *Gaslight* is a George Cukor thriller set in Victorian London, about a young woman slowly and methodically driven mad by her manipulative, murderous husband. Hedy Lamarr had reportedly turned down the meaty role, but Bergman actively went after it, campaigning to be loaned to MGM for the chance to play a character who struggles to hold on to her sanity and control while slowly coming apart. Her efforts paid off; Ingrid Bergman won her first Oscar for a phenomenal performance.

The film is based on the play, *Gas Light* (1938) by Patrick Hamilton, and was preceded by the British film adaptation, *Gaslight* (1940). It had also been previously on the stage in Broadway as *Angel Street* in 1941. The term "gaslighting" has since been popularly used as a type of psychological abuse, where a victim is driven to question their perception of reality by a manipulator who in turn gains more power and control

Speaking of altered perceptions… the statuesque height of Ingrid Bergman, who stands tall at 5'9", required her co-star, Charles Boyer, to stand on a box for some of their scenes together. Actress Angela Lansbury, who made her debut in the film, had to make adjustments for the lead star's towering height too; she had to wear high platform shoes. It wasn't just Ingrid Bergman's height that gave her a domineering presence. She had always tended to be on the big-boned side, which met with the occasional commentary of being hefty or somewhat overweight. It was one of the reasons she found solace in acting; in real life, she had once said, she felt "*too big and clumsy.*" But on a stage? "*I can do everything with ease.*"

- **The Bells of St. Mary's (1945)**. She took on lighter, more wholesome fare with Leo McCarey's *The Bells of St. Mary's* (1945), which she starred in with Bing Crosby. It's a film unlike Bergman's usual heavier outputs, a sequel to boot (of *Going My Way* (1944)), and one she had to make a case with David O. Selznick to allow her to do over at RKO. She reportedly wanted to display her range and versatility with something unexpected.

  In this film, Bergman plays Sister Benedict, the young, kind-hearted but stubborn nun running a deteriorating inner-city Catholic school, St. Mary's. She tangles with Bing's happy-go-lucky singing priest, Father O'Malley, a recent transfer. They are both sympathetic characters with vastly different approaches to the running of the school.

Bergman's instincts were spot on in fighting to do the film. Her performance was calm but layered, and she was entrancing in it. The movie was a crowd and critic pleaser; it was nominated for eight Academy Awards, including Best Director, Best Actor and Best Actress. It became not only the top-grossing film of 1945 – but also (adjusted for current values of course) in the top grossing films of all time in the domestic market.

- **Notable Films with Alfred Hitchcock.**
Ingrid Bergman was a self-possessed, independent woman who sought out creative challenges and admired men with skills and vision. She was also a beautiful woman who could turn up a nuanced performance. And so it should not be so surprising that her career path would cross that of gifted but notoriously difficult filmmaker, Alfred Hitchcock. She found him overly prepared; a trait that was impressive but also had its cons, because it came at the cost of a director's willingness to collaborate with and be receptive to the inputs of his actors. Nevertheless, Bergman and Hitchcock would work together on three films and were said to be lifelong friends.

First amongst their collaborations was *Spellbound* (1945), loosely based on the novel, *The House of Dr. Edwardes* by Francis Beeding. Here, Bergman plays psychoanalyst, Dr. Constance Petersen, who falls in love with an amnesiac accused of murder (played by Gregory Peck). Convinced he is innocent and that the answers are hiding in puzzles somewhere within his broken mind, she takes it upon herself to get to the bottom of the crime via psychoanalysis. The crowd-pleasing mystery was nominated for several Oscars. It is also notable for the involvement of iconic surrealist painter, Salvador Dali, who had worked on art for a dream sequence.

The romantic spy thriller, *Notorious*, followed in 1946. Ingrid Bergman played Alicia Huberman, the guilt-ridden, American-born daughter of a German spy. Alicia is used by Cary Grant's embittered American agent, T.R. Devlin, to infiltrate a cadre of Nazi expats in South America and foil their plans. Bergman made a convincing double agent, entangling her handler and her Nazi target in a love triangle. She thrilled audiences by her believable and attractive performance. The only person who might have been displeased by Bergman? Hitchcock's indispensable, long-suffering wife, Alma Reville, for Hitchcock was rumored to be infatuated with his film's luminous leading lady at the time of filming. *Notorious* is essential viewing for Hitchcock fans too, for the auteur's signature themes – complex female identity, dysfunctional mother-child relationships and the narrative device, "MacGuffin" - are seen here in their early forms.

The last of their films together was the technically ambitious but ultimately unremarkable, *Under Capricorn* (1949), which is not quite regarded as the best of either Bergman or Hitchcock, but mentioned here to round up the scope of their collaborations. It was beautiful to look at but a box office bomb, which was eventually lost amid the Bergman – Rossellini scandal.

- **Notable Films with Roberto Rossellini.**
Ingrid Bergman had reportedly seen
Italian, neorealist director, Roberto
Rossellini's work in *Open City* and *Paisan*,
and was so moved as to write him a letter
offering her talents. *Stromboli* (1950) was
his earnest proposal in response. The
couple would eventually work on a
number of films together – none very
successful - but it was *Stromboli* that
started it all. In this heartfelt drama,
Bergman plays Karin, a war refugee who
thought she found salvation in marriage
to an Italian fisherman. When he brought
her to the traditional island of the film's
title, the beautiful, transplanted outsider
instead found mounting isolation and
descent into despair. It was poorly
received on account of the scandal

between the director and his star, but even on its own merits it was divisive; some considered it beautiful, others found it utterly depressing and worse, boring. Perhaps it was all three at some point or another. Either way, it is still counted as a must-see for Ingrid Bergman and Roberto Rossellini fans, especially as there is more and more belated appreciation for the film.

Of the movies the controversial couple made together, *Journey to Italy* (1954) is often considered to be the best of the bunch. Here, Bergman plays one half of a wealthy English couple caught in a decaying relationship. After eight years of marriage, Katherine (Bergman's role) and Alex (played by George Sanders) are vacationing in Italy but the trip only magnifies their unhappiness, dissatisfaction, disappointment and lack of shared vision or purpose.

Journey to Italy is considered by some to be a particularly personal film for Bergman and Rossellini, whose union could be contentious – they were having personal and professional problems as their works were poorly received - and eventually it did decay to an end. Some Hollywood pundits have even remarked on it as somewhat autobiographical, with Sanders' physical resemblance to Rossellini. Of course, any film that starred the director's spouse, whether or not they had marital challenges, would have a personal quality. But it would have been more marked given the kind of approach Rossellini had with filmmaking. As a director, he had been described as idiosyncratic and almost unprofessional compared with what Bergman was more used to in Hollywood. He did not work with actors from a formal script, and he welcomed heavy improvisation. Bergman had once described Rossellini as akin to a war general, and that he was the only one who knew *"what the soldiers were supposed to do."* He would cast non-actors. In *Stromboli*, an Oscar-winning actress of Bergman's caliber had to work with amateurs who, if accounts hold true, needed strings tied to their big toes pulled for their cue!

Rossellini was also willing to conjure real and sometimes dangerous off-screen emotions on the set, if it helped fulfill his creative vision. Bergman was able to adjust (eventually), but her *Journey to Italy* leading man, George Sanders, was driven to nervous breakdowns by the Rossellini style – which, rather maddeningly, may have been intentional. Sanders was billeted in a different hotel from everyone else, and the actors were reportedly told to steer away from him. According to a Rossellini biographer, the director seemed to be actively creating feelings of isolation in the star so that Sanders' tension and anguish would show in the character.

The poor performance of their films together – their collaborations include *Europe '51* (1952); *Siamo donne* (1953); and *Fear* (1954) - gave rise to a myth that Roberto Rossellini had somewhat of a curse on Ingrid Bergman but the truth is, she's had Hollywood disappointments before they were married too, such as *Joan of Arc* (1948), *Arch of Triumph* (1948) and *Under Capricorn* (1949). These failures, along with her dissatisfaction with Hollywood roles, was actually one of the reasons why she sought our Roberto Rossellini in the first place. She wanted a challenge, and the versatility that she hoped would further her career.

- *Anastasia* **(1956).** *Anastasia* saw Ingrid Bergman returning to Hollywood with aplomb. It was a movie about an exile finding her way back home – a fitting, fighting role for a screen queen's Hollywood homecoming.

In *Anastasia*, the hunt is on for the Grand Duchess Anastasia, the near-mythical sole survivor of the Bolshevik radicals' massacre of the ruling Romanov family of Russia in 1918. Over the succeeding years, rumors of one of Tsar Nicholas' daughters' dramatic escape captivates pretenders and opportunists who want to profit from the tragedy, and distresses surviving family members with false hopes. The movie, set ten years after the killings, finds Bergman's amnesiac vagrant Anna in the grip of an ambitious former Russian General (played by Yul Brynner). General Bounine believes he and his cohorts can profit from passing her off as the long-lost Grand Duchess, if they can package her correctly and play their cards right. But over the course of their work together, Anna displays intimate knowledge of the Romanov life – leading to the question, could she in fact be the real Anastasia?

The story was based on the real-life of Anna Anderson, who came to fame over her royal claims. Marcelle Maurette did a play on the tale in France in 1951, and Guy Bolton had a hit on his hands in 1954 when he made a Broadway adaptation. Many studios made a play for the film rights, and it would be 20th Century Fox to win the contest. Director Anatole Litvak and studio head Daryl F. Zanuck made a case for Ingrid Bergman in the lead.

Bergman gives the epic premise a touching human quality. There is fame, money and glamour, but her expressive acting never lets us forget the human cost of loss, mental illness, and the very real tragedy behind the romantic notion of a long-lost princess. She deservedly brought home the Academy's Best Actress in a Leading Role award for her moving performance. But more than bringing home the industry's most coveted award, in Hollywood, she was actually *home*. She belonged before the camera and admired. She not only continued to work on television and the movies afterwards, but the town had one more Academy Award to honor her with in the future.

- *Murder on the Orient Express* **(1974)**. Sidney Lumet's star-studded film adaptation of the beloved Agatha Christie mystery is a charming crowd-pleaser, featuring the likes of Albert Finney as the eccentric, genius detective, Hercule Poirot and big names like Lauren Bacall and Sean Connery. Aboard the Orient Express, Poirot faces a fancy train full of suspects in a brutal on-board murder. Bergman plays Greta, a flustered, nervous missionary – one of many under suspicion for the crime. She stood out even in a sea of stars, and won the Academy Award for Best Actress in a Supporting Role.

- ***Autumn Sonata* (1978).** *Autumn Sonata* brought Ingrid Bergman and the (unrelated) filmmaker, Ingmar Bergman together in this film, about the complex ties between a neglectful mother (Bergman) and her now-adult daughter (played by Liv Ullman) who wants to forge a reconnection. Their interactions start out pleasant enough, but unravels to show cracks and strain and even resentment. Bergman's powerful performance here, delivered raw and without vanity, is considered one of her best, in a career of bests… and it unfortunately mirrored some elements of her real life.

  The searing portrayal handed Ingrid Bergman the final Academy Award nomination of her storied career. It could have been her final role too, which she is said to have considered at the time. "*I don't want to go down and play little parts*," she had once said, in consideration of perhaps ending her filmography here. Small parts and short engagements had been uninteresting to her, even if there was still a demand for her talents at her age. Luckily for her adoring audience, she appeared in one more project, and still in the lead role – for *A Woman Called Golda* on television.

- **Notable Broadway Appearances.** Ingrid Bergman was a versatile actress who also graced the live stage. She was in Ferenc Molnar's *Liliom* (1940); in Eugene O'Neill's *More Stately Mansions* (1967); in

George Bernard Shaw's *Captain Brassbound's Conversion* (1972); W. Somerset Maugham's *The Constant Wife* (1975); and of course, in Maxwell Anderson's *Joan of Lorraine* (1946) – for which she took home the stage's coveted Tony award for Best Actress in a Play.

The premise of *Joan of Lorraine* is that an actress slated to play Joan of Arc, Mary Grey (played by Bergman) finds herself at odds with her colleagues on the direction the characterization should take. It was a play-within-a-play, which was an interesting approach to the classic story of the celebrated French heroine. When it was brought to the screens with Ingrid Bergman playing Joan and Maxwell Anderson's work still contributing to the script, they played it more straightforwardly, keeping only the historical tale. *Joan of Arc* (1948) did not do very well in the box office, but it would hand Bergman another acting nomination from the Academy, which had also given the film two wins and six nominations on other categories.

- **Notable Television Appearances.** Like many of her contemporaries, Ingrid Bergman shared her talents on the small screen too. The medium of television increasingly became a part of the national lifestyle after World War II, when home ownership increased, suburban living grew, and television set purchases rose. Box office attendance was slowing down, as it required more cost and effort to go to cinemas in town. There was a wide variety of material available to television audiences, and many of Hollywood's familiar faces played in the sandbox of this new medium.

Ingrid Bergman appeared on television series and made-for-TV movies and asserted her domination here too; she has an Emmy for Outstanding Single Performance By an Actress for an episode of *Startime* (1959), a Ford Motor Company-sponsored variety, musical and dramatic program. She featured in an adaptation of *The Turn of the Screw*, where she plays a governess who may or may not be haunted by her predecessor. Bergman also has an Emmy for Outstanding Lead Actress in a Limited

Series or a Special, for the biopic, *A Woman Called Golda* (1982). She had already been very ill while it was filming, but the actress was determined to maximize the time she had left and what she enjoyed most was her work. She was not certain she could go through the rigors of filming, but in the end, she found herself enriched "*as an actress and a human being*" who was able to get "*more out of life than expected.*"

In *A Woman Called Golda*, she played iconic Israeli prime minister, Golda Meir. According to a producer on the series, Bergman was often in pain and had to sleep with a traction for her hand to avoid swelling. She always gave effort but somehow made her performances so natural. *A Woman Called Golda* was her final screen credit.

Ingrid Bergman had great passion, some would even say compulsion, for her craft. She was a professional, always prepared, a good presence both in front of and behind the scenes. She took it seriously and actively sought out challenging parts to play. She wanted to show her versatility, and was gutsy about taking on even unglamorous, unflattering roles. Even in her success she also showed humility, and she was famous for saying after takes that if she did more, she would be *"better later."*

She was an intelligent performer, with courage, conviction and a sense of collaboration. She was an amazing actress, with a talent and personality that could rise, phoenix-like, from the ashes of a scandal that rocked both Hollywood and Washington.

The Woman

Ingrid Bergman could be very philosophical about acting. She was always an intelligent, straightforward woman who could speak with a lot of thought and passion for it.

She had, for example, spoke of how she liked changing "*as much as possible*" when it came to playing parts. While many of her early roles had a distinct sense of moral uprightness about them (in *Intermezzo*, *Casablanca*, *For Whom the Bell Tolls*, *Gaslight*, *The Bells of St. Mary's*, *Spellbound* and *Joan of Arc*), she was also active in seeking out different kinds of roles and had shown willingness to fight and campaign for a meaty part. She was a self-aware performer and knew what kind of saintly image she had, which she reportedly agonized over, for everyone had "*shades of bad and good*" in them.

One of the most famous quotes attributed to her, perfectly illustrates her level-headed, pragmatic approach to her craft, her image, and her personal life: "*I don't think anyone has the right to intrude in your life, but they do. I would like people to separate the actress and the woman.*"

And as a woman, she did have shades of "bad -" just like everyone else. It's just that no one else is expected to be as saintly as she was, for a time, expected to be. She had a complicated personal life, with its affairs and broken relationships.

The Lindstrom-Bergman-Rossellini Triangle

When a man is the injured party in one of the biggest scandals of the 1950s, it is an unfortunate truth that he would be most commonly remembered as being Ingrid Bergman's first husband, rather than a person of considerable achievements on his own. But Dr. Petter Lindstrom, who was married to Bergman for 13 years, was also his own man.

Lindstrom, a native of Sweden, had a doctorate for dental surgery and a private practice in Stockholm in the early 1930s. He was also an educator at the Karolinska Institiute. He was eight years Ingrid's senior and already accomplished when they met, reportedly when she was 18 years old and agreed to go with her cousin on a group date. He was handsome, smart, and had a good sense of humor alongside a traditional set of values. They married shortly after her star-making *Intermezzo*. By 1939, they had their first child, a daughter named Pia. It was a time of change; she was a new mother, yes, but Hollywood, via David O. Selznick, was also knocking on the Swedish star's door.

Bergman headed off to Hollywood. Lindstrom and their daughter followed a few months afterwards. They settled in Beverly Hills and their respective stars rose together. Over the next few years he became a neurosurgeon and she brought home her first Oscar. Their home life seemed ideal, except behind the scenes (so to speak), that was not necessarily the case.

Lindstrom, as was later revealed, could be domineering. Bergman, on the other hand, would also be revealed as somewhat selfishly driven especially with her acting. He was said to be critical and overly frugal. She was said to be heavy on the drinking and had a wandering eye. It was increasingly clear they had different approaches to life, and she reportedly wanted a divorce that he, by preference or strict values, did not want to give.

If accounts are true, the married couple actually saw Italian neorealist director, Roberto Rossellini's *Rome, Open City* (1945) together. It was one of the works that had touched Bergman to such an extent that she felt a deep desire to work with the director. She wrote him and offered her talents. He would offer up *Stromboli* in return.

Roberto Rossellini was born on the 18th of May, 1906, in Rome. He was from a well-to-do family, headed by his father, who built movie theaters in the city. The family thus had networks and inroads to the Italian film industry, and Rossellini as well as a younger brother would eventually make their living there. Roberto worked his way up and had dabbled in a miscellany of tasks relating to filmmaking. But he was an artist caught in a complex period of world history.

Benito Mussolini believed in the power of cinema in shaping public perceptions and Italian cinema was very productive in his fascist regime. In this context, we find the nascent talent of Roberto Rossellini. His profession eventually saw him assisting filmmaker Francesco De Robertis, who had been in charge of the Fascist government's film service for the country's navy. They made a number of projects, including features on submarines and ships. Rossellini was also said to be good friends with Benito Mussolini's son, Vittorio, who was influential in helping him direct what cinephiles would later call his "Fascist Trilogy - " propaganda films *The White Ship* (1941), *A Pilot Returns* (1942), and *The Man With the Cross* (1943). It was government propaganda, but elements of his later signature style would be found here – an almost documentary format, contemporary characters, settings and issues, authentic location filming and the use of amateur actors.

Around midway through World War II, Italy shifted sides and surrendered to Allied forces, which moved its former collaborator, Germany, to occupy sections of its territory including Rome. During this tumultuous time, Rossellini hid to avoid being conscripted. He shared an apartment with screenwriter Sergio Amidei and a resistance fighter. These are the ingredients that would eventually comprise his masterpiece, *Rome, Open City*. Rossellini was the director, Amidei one of the screenwriters, and they were both caught in the experience of an occupied city and exposed to resistance activities.

Rossellini was determined to make the film, and barely two months from the liberation of Rome, he and his crew were shooting on the streets in authentic locations, selling their belongings to purchase film and buying necessities on the black market – even before World War II ended. When it came out, the film picked up slowly but eventually, *Rome, Open City* and Rossellini came into the success and renown they deserved. The film, and *Paisan* (1946) to follow it, helped popularize neorealist cinema.

The films made their way before the eyes of Ingrid Bergman and Petter Lindstrom and by 1948, Rossellini was meeting with the couple in the United States at the Lindstrom home to discuss options for a project together. *Stromboli* and the biggest scandal of their time was slowly brewing.

At this time, Bergman was dissatisfied by the roles Hollywood was laying at her feet. She was also dissatisfied with her marriage. This, coupled by her falling into the sphere of romantic Rossellini's genius and vitality, contributed to their extramarital affair. Bergman and Rossellini fell in love while filming – in spite of the rugged work environment, Rossellini's uncommon approach, and the exhausting and emotionally draining shoot. She soon became pregnant. Bergman informed her husband she would not be coming home. She appealed for a divorce and to see their child, but Petter Lindstrom denied his erring wife both requests.

Rossellini and Bergman courted moral outrage beyond that of her cuckolded husband. Ire came their way from seemingly every corner of the entire United States. The scandal of their off-screen romance while filming *Stromboli* was likely exacerbated by Bergman's saintly, morally-upright public image. She has played a nun – and reportedly inspired many young girls to the nunnery. She has played Joan of Arc. And everyone believed that with her accomplished husband and 10-year-old daughter, she had a stable family life.

The affair created a huge public outcry from many corners. Bergman got a scathing response from the United States by virtue of failed, lofty expectations on her saintliness but Rossellini, while already a notorious figure, wouldn't be exempt either. He was married too but separated from Marcella de Marchis, but this hardly made him "free" to pursue a new romance. He already had a mistress, the beloved star of *Rome, Open City*, the sultry Anna Magnani. Magnani is said to have been set aside from *Stromboli* to make way for the Hollywood superstar and Rossellini's new lover, Ingrid Bergman. The scandal threw labels like "*love pirate*" and "*home wrecker*" Rossellini's way, and his past also led him to be described as a *"Nazi collaborator"* and *"black market operator."*

For a while there, he and Bergman made a rather unpopular couple, but they moved forward as they had to. She gave birth to their first child, Robertino, out of wedlock in 1950. A week afterwards, she secured a Mexican proxy divorce and she and her director lover were soon free to marry. They exchanged vows in May, 1950. She and Lindstrom were granted a firmer divorce later that year, and custody of their daughter Pia would go to Petter.

In Europe, Bergman and Rossellini had what has been described as a short honeymoon period before their relationship began to deteriorate, too. They had two other children after Robertino, the twins Isabella and Isotta. They continued to work together too, though unfortunately, they found no salvation nor lasting comfort from successful creative outputs. Because Bergman settled down in Europe away from the furor and steered well-clear of Hollywood for years, they had fewer filmmaking opportunities and worked together heavily. They were reasonably prolific but not very successful commercially or critically. Though this perspective would change over the years – history would show many of the movies as works of art with a distinct cinematic vision, inviting rediscovery, and Ingrid Bergman would always stand by their work - this did not help them at the time.

The "failure" of the films (even if they would be appreciated by later cinephiles), was attributed to a fundamental mismatch between a larger-than-life Hollywood star and a neorealist director. Rossellini had once been quoted as saying that *"A star cannot help being a star…"* in that the films that they made together were not what her public expected of her, and having someone like her in them was not what his audience expected of him. He did semi-documentaries; she was an actress and entertainer. But she was in a sense, "stuck" working with him while effectively banned in Hollywood, and he, with her. A middle-point between their polar opposite core strengths became lukewarm for their fanbases. Their styles did not seem to suit.

Their failures would have been hard enough to bear, but they had different temperaments too, on top of Rossellini's mercurial personality, possessiveness (he was allegedly against her working with other filmmakers), careless spending, and unfaithfulness. It was this last that had finally cut their ties, though they've been strained for years. When he became entangled with another woman, Ingrid Bergman mentioned in her diary that she "*felt strangely relieved.*"

While Roberto Rossellini was working with the Indian Films Division under invitation from Jawaharlal Nehru himself, he had an affair with Sonali Dasgupta – his producer's wife (the two later married). Bergman and Rossellini separated in 1957 and their marriage was eventually annulled. Bergman won custody of their children.

Ingrid Bergman was free, but far from rudderless. With a single, moving performance, she reclaimed her place in Hollywood. She filmed *Anastasia* in Europe under the direction of Anatole Litvak, and returned to Tinsel Town with a resounding bang. But Ingrid Bergman did not return cowed, like Hollywood's prodigal child. She returned like a conqueror and she took no prisoners – she won over critics. She took back her public. She even brought home the coveted Oscar.

Lars Schmidt

Of her handful of marriages, Ingrid Bergman described what she had with Swedish theatrical producer and businessman, Lars Schmidt, as being the strongest. They married in 1958. They shared personality traits, as well as a love for theater. According to one of Ingrid Bergman's interviews, it was the demands of work that broke the union. Spending so much time apart eventually led them to divorce. Another account has Schmidt being unfaithful and getting his mistress pregnant. Either way, he was still with her when she died in London in 1982, even after they have been divorced since 1975.

Alleged Affairs

Ingrid Bergman was later revealed to have a wandering eye which allegedly targeted actor Spencer Tracey, with whom she starred in *Dr. Jekyll and Mr. Hyde* (1941); Victor Fleming who had directed her on the same film as well as in *Joan of Arc*; Gary Cooper, with whom she was cast in *For Whom the Bell Tolls*; musician Larry Adler; and legendary war photographer, Robert Capa. Gregory Peck, for one had reportedly admitted to a fling when they were filming Alfred Hitchcock's *Spellbound*. How much the rest of these men may have reciprocated on the attentions of the dreamy Bergman is unknown. The greater mystery though, is that who would have been able to resist her?

Children

Ingrid Bergman has been described as selfishly driven, especially when it came to her craft and career. By her actions, it could be surmised that she had often prioritized acting over family. Her trip to Hollywood after being lured by Selznick to make the American version of *Intermezzo*, for example, had been without her then-husband, Petter Lindstrom, and their newborn Pia. When she took up her romance with Roberto Rossellini during the filming of *Stromboli*, she had left them behind, too. She had asked Petter for contact with Pia but had reportedly been denied. Bergman was dealt a particularly harsh blow when she lost custody of her, and the reunion between mother and daughter wouldn't be until years later. By then, Pia was reportedly 18, and even after all that time, their meeting was still against the wishes of the still-embittered Petter.

Petter Lindstrom would go on to teach and practice medicine in prestigious institutions, become a famous brain surgeon, re-marry (he was married for 45 years!) and have more children and grandchildren who adored him. He would even outlive Bergman by many years, passing away in 2000, at the age of 93. But he was never quite able to fully absolve Ingrid Bergman of her faults in the Rossellini affair. He would later reveal his troubles with the Hollywood legend, whom he described as a heavy smoker and drinker, and who had been neglectful of her children.

Towards the last few years of Ingrid Bergman's life, she had admitted to feeling guilt about where she had placed her priorities, but was candid enough to say, she was also *"not guilty enough to stop working."* Indeed, Ingrid Bergman was not very big on regrets. She had once been asked if she harbored them about the choices she made in life. She said, *"I regret the things I didn't do."* She did, however, express guilt about how her romance with Rossellini had affected and pained Pia.

She had four children. Pia, by Petter Lindstrom, would eventually become a famous personality. She was on television for three decades and is still active in the entertainment industry via a radio show, *Pia Lindstrom Presents*, and through member and/or trusteeship roles with the Theater

Development Fund, American Theater Wing and the Tony Award Nominating Committee. She has two Emmy Awards for her work in TV journalism.

Renato Robertino or Robin, her first child by Rossellini and born in Italy before she and the director could marry, became a handsome businessman who at one time became romantically linked with Her Serene Highness, Princess Caroline of Monaco.

Bergman also had twins by Rossellini, Isotta ("Ingrid" in Italian); and Isabella. Isotta became a professor for Italian Literature at New York University. Isabella would become a model, marry and split from iconic director Martin Scorsese, and become a successful actress on her own merits. As of this writing, she has 85 screen credits to her name, and has also been nominated at the Golden Globe Awards and Emmy Awards.

Isabella, who had been a sickly child, could claim more contact with their mother than her siblings. When Pia was young, her mother was in larger demand and building her career. They were also separated after Ingrid and Petter split up amid the Rossellini affair. But by the time Isabella came along, there was less demands on Ingrid Bergman's time, which had been fortunate, because Isabella needed her mother often at her side. She had a spinal deformity that necessitated operations and extensive care; Ingrid Bergman, she fondly recalled in an interview, *was the perfect nurse.*

Ingrid Bergman's children seemed to have emerged well-adjusted in spite of their mother's alleged neglect, admitted de-prioritization of family that led her to live away from them frequently and for stretches of time, and her complex public and personal life. When she passed away in 1982, she had left no instructions on how to split her valuables amongst them and the siblings managed to amicably make arrangements on their own. After all, on Academy Awards alone, they had plenty to share amongst themselves.

Legacy

Ingrid Bergman had a long battle with cancer. She had been diagnosed around the time she was cast on *Murder on the Orient Express* in 1973, and had a mastectomy in 1974 and another in 1979. But she always kept herself busy. In the 1970s, she could still be spotted drawing in crowds on stage and screen, and in 1980 she published an autobiography, *Ingrid Bergman: My Story*. She had an active, engaged life right up to her last role, that of Golda Meir in *A Woman Called Golda* in the early 1980s. That doesn't, however, mean that it was easy. She filmed while in constant pain.

Here, her courage and fortitude shown alongside her talents. She had been of the belief that if one does not learn to live with the disease, cancer can destroy the time she had left. And so, one must try and get used to it, and hold onto things that are more important. Illness should not prevent one from enjoying what remained of life. For her, that enjoyment included performing.

Ingrid Bergman had always known she was a good actress, but she also had her feet on the ground. She had a pragmatic humility and desire for constant improvement about her craft, and in her last film set, she was nervous because before *A Woman Called Golda*, her last film credit had been *Autumn Sonata* all the way back in 1978. What she found comfort in was the camera, and in motioning towards one she had reportedly said, "*but I see a friend over there.*"

She loved the camera and performing in front of it. Her late, beloved father had really shared his passion for visual arts with her and she would have it all her life. Furthermore, in performance she found solace; if in real life she found herself somewhat larger than others and ungainly, her fears and hesitations vanished on the stage. It was also comfort and escape from loneliness when she was a child without siblings, and then as an orphan. Her pursuit of creative challenge, even at big costs to her personal life, brought her to interesting places and led her to make unforgettable films in iconic roles, with the legendary talents of het time. No wonder she found few reasons to regret her choices.

Indeed, she had a great love for the camera and as everyone knows, it loved her right back. In any age, in any role, in black and white or color, she shone. Film captured her incandescence, inner radiance and natural luminosity with ease, and translated it so well such that even decades after her death, she can still captivate.

She died of cancer at age 67 on her birthday, the 29th of August 1982.

She left behind a legacy unmatched by any of her actress peers, not only by her beauty and talent, but by her bold, adventurous choices and desire for constant change and development, which brought her to all sorts of media. She was in the movies, of course, with three Oscars to show her dominance of it. But she was also an award-winning stage and television performer, and she found as much joy in these other media too. She reportedly liked the immediacy of a thousand eyes presented by the theater, but she also liked the frenzy of a television schedule. In film, she was as great on a well-controlled Hollywood set as she was on location at a volcanic crater in Roberto Rossellini's gritty, neorealist projects. She left the world with a stunning body of work linguistically as well; she worked in two continents and five languages!

Aside from her official filmography, she also left the world with a stunning collection of documentation on her life. She kept records exhaustively. She had a diary, which may have helped ease her loneliness as a child and writing in it was something she kept up for a long time. She kept letters, too. She also had an astounding amount of home movies and photographs, likely another influence of her father.

Isabella Rossellini reportedly remembered asking her mother why she had bothered with record-keeping so much, which would have been challenging in her various moves; the actress had called Sweden, the United States, Italy, France and England home at one point or another, after all. Ingrid Bergman's response was uncharacteristically confident for a woman who tended toward quiet strength and humility – she knew her life was important.

Here her creative instincts proved right, again. A lot of her personally-kept records would be used in a 2015 feature-length, *Ingrid Bergman: In Her Own Words* by Swedish director, Stig Bjorkman, alongside interviews from family and friends. It premiered in Cannes in 2015, to wide acclaim.

The documentary is just one of the ways the world celebrated her life on her centennial.

The Museum of Modern Art hosted a 14-film retrospective with her daughters introducing them. The Brooklyn Academy of Music also hosted tribute screenings in 2015. Across the seas, there was "A Tribute to Ingrid" at London's Royal Festival Hall, and another tribute at the Theatre du Chatelet in Paris. These are only a few ways the world showed it continues to treasure the talents Ingrid Bergman shared while she was alive. She was a true internationally beloved actress.

In the letter that began her working (and otherwise) relationship with Roberto Rossellini, she had described herself as "*a Swedish actress who speaks English very well, who has not forgotten her German, who is not very understandable in French, and who in Italian knows only 'ti amo…'*"

It seems that at whatever level of proficiency, in every language she spoke, she was a talent. And the moment Ingrid Bergman says "*Ti amo*," no one could resist saying "I love you" right back. As an actress and as a woman, on the screen and off of it, from the men and art she loved, she was and continues to be loved in return.

Grace Kelly

True Stories of a
Psychological
Phenomenon

Dr. Julia Sanders

Copyright © 2017.

All rights reserved. No part of this publication may be reproduced, distributed, or transmitted in any form or by any means, including photocopying, recording, or other electronic or mechanical methods, without the prior written permission of the publisher, except in the case of brief quotations embodied in critical reviews and certain other noncommercial uses permitted by copyright law.

This book is intended for informational and entertainment purposes only. The publisher limits all liability arising from this work to the fullest extent of the law.

Table of Contents

Grace Kelly –The Anti-Cinderella

Introduction

Whenever one hears of a prince finding a bride without royal blood, inevitably, the term "Cinderella" pops up. On one side, a wealthy, handsome prince in search of love. On the other, a guileless, virginal, anonymous woman of lower station, "common" but with a wholly uncommon beauty and charm. She sweeps him off his feet. They fall in love. He moves heaven and earth to find her. They marry and live happily ever after.

In the case of Grace Kelly – Hollywood beauty turned Her Serene Highness, Princess Consort of Monaco after her well-publicized, well-packaged storybook marriage to Prince Rainier III – the Cinderella reference is easy to make, but far from accurate. All too many key points of the narrative just are not there.

For one thing, Prince Charming had a complex lineage that counted among his relations, the daughter of a laundress. He was also heir to a kingdom that was floundering in economic problems, and under threat from its powerful neighbors and competitors. Whether he had intended it or not – for some rumors do suggest Rainier might have been actively seeking a marketable American bride – the Prince's marriage to a superstar was one way of putting his little principality on the world map and setting his grand plans for its revival into motion. Thus, in this fairy tale? There may have been love, but there could have also been the less romantic notion of function.

Second, the "Cinderella" of our tale was neither anonymous nor needy – Grace Kelly was a successful Hollywood actress and an Academy Award winner, yes, but she had also come from a wealthy Philadelphia family. Ever heard of Cinderella paying a $2 million dowry to marry her Prince Charming? Well that is what the Kellys had to do when their daughter Grace married Rainier III. Reportedly, her family footed half of the money and she was successful enough to handle the rest herself.

As for guileless and virginal... Hollywood's reigning ice queen had a beautiful, stony countenance but she was a passionate conqueror underneath. She was rumored to be a heartbreaker, a man-eater who went through not only plenty a leading man, but she didn't even spare the married ones.

More importantly? When Rainier III married Grace Kelly, he did not quite elevate her to his station. They had something more of a partnership. He may have given her a title and a position, but she was instrumental in elevating the image of his country by her name and innate glamour. She was the one who made her new position modern, relevant and enviable. She made "Princess of Monaco" mean something fresh and extraordinary. Monaco, at the time, was somewhat in decline and has also been known as 'a sunny country for shady people.' But simply because *the* Grace Kelly was its Princess, there was something about the locale that was elegant and desirable. In so many ways, she became ambassadorial.

The "Cinderella" connection would be inaccurate for one more reason – happily ever after was all too temporary. Grace Kelly's life was cut short by a car accident in 1982. The Princess was only 53 at the time, much too young and still so beautiful. As of this writing, the country she had made her home still stands, also beautiful and still prosperous, but not immune from scandal. The beautiful royal family she left behind have all been caught in each of their own controversies.

Her son, Prince Albert II, fathered illegitimate children with different women when he was a bachelor. Just before his wedding in 2011, the family had to deny rumors that his wife-to-be, Charlene Whittstock, was caught at the airport trying to flee – it was just one of several alleged escape attempts she was trying to make to after realizing the extent of his indiscretions.

Prince Rainier and Princess Grace's daughters, Caroline and Stephanie, have complicated love lives of their own. Caroline has married thrice; one ending in divorce, another ending in a tragic death, and her current one at an estrangement with a troubled man. Stephanie, on the other hand, had marriages and divorces with her bodyguard and a trapeze artist. She also has several children conceived out of wedlock.

Ironically, Princess Grace's children mired in a series of romantic misfortunes might be one of the few, vaguely aspects of Grace

Kelly's story resembling a fairy tale – for if family lore holds true, a curse was once set upon the Grimaldis wherein they would never have real happiness in marriage. If this holds true, then Albert II< Carlone and Stephanie may just be the most recent casualties in a line long plagued by romantic scandal and tragedy. This curse would also be blamed for the Princess' untimely death, by people who may believe in such things. Whether or not one subscribes to this belief is immaterial. Perhaps there is a curse afoot, perhaps it is simply a way of attempting to understand the seemingly improbable number of romantic hardships borne by a single family. Either way, early death and a troubled family life are hardly anyone's idea of happily-ever-after.

In this and in many ways, Grace Kelly is the anti-Cinderella. She is made no less beautiful and no less glamorous by this, however. If anything, her depth and complexity, and how she and her family have tried to weather the storms in their lives, makes them even more interesting and worthy of knowing.

Early Life

Grace Patricia Kelly was born on the 12th of November, 1929, in Philadelphia, Pennsylvania. She was one of John Brendan "Jack" Kelly, and Margaret Katherine Majer's four children – one boy and three girls. Grace was the ill-fitting middle daughter.

Jack and Margaret were very athletic. He was a three-time gold medalist for the United States' Olympic rowing team, and is in the U.S. Olympic Hall of Fame. She was a champion collegiate swimmer, and in University of Pennsylvania, she was a physical education instructor and the Ivy League school's the first coach for the women's teams. The Kelly family was prosperous not for their feats in sports, however. Jack was a self-made millionaire, the son of an immigrant bricklayer and a former laborer himself, turned contractor who owned a lucrative brick business in the East Coast. He had even built the family's stately, 2 and 1/2 –story brick, Georgian mansion in Philadelphia. It had a playhouse and a tennis court, which in the winters were iced over for skating.

Jack had his eyes set not only on financial success but establishing himself and his family within their well-heeled community. He worked hard, but was also busy with sports and politics. One of his political achievements was to be elected into the City Council. He had grand dreams for his children, too, and he and his wife had an intense style of motivating them. The Kelly parents were hard to please and encouraged competition among the siblings – allegedly, competing even for the love of mom and dad. The Kellys required discipline and obedience, and though they employed household servants, the children were still expected to help with chores. Margaret in particular had a reputation as a disciplinarian, and had been described as not averse to using the rod on the Kelly children.

Education for a privileged Philadelphia girl like Grace Kelly started with the Sisters of the Assumption's all-girls Catholic school, Ravenhill Academy. She then went on to Stevens School, a private high school.

Grace Kelly as she is most famously remembered, is a slim blond with chiseled features, immaculate hair and chic clothes.

Her look was carefully cultivated, celestial, and in the words of her frequent film collaborator, the legendary Alfred Hitchcock, she had *"sexual elegance."* But in her younger years, this dreamy, immortal image of a stylish femme fatale was a lifetime away. She was a little bit on the heavy side, with glasses and a small bust. She had a thin, nasal voice. She was shy. But she eventually grew into the unabashed beauty she was always meant to be, and acting only buffered up her confidence. She had a real passion for it, and participated in productions within her East Falls, Philadelphia community on top of being in school plays. At The Little Theater in their upscale neighborhood, she participated in performances from the early age of 12 (some reports even say she started at 10). She also did some modeling and fashion events. Eventually, she never lacked for attention or admiration from young men.

Much harder to please were her parents. The Kelly household prized athletic achievement, and indeed, home movies of the four kids – a brother, Grace and her two sisters – would show them leaping from rooftops and racing. Her brother John Jr. would even go on to become an Olympic medalist himself. Grace, however, wasn't quite like her family and she did not have much of a heart for competitive sports. She was also sickly, and her nasal voice is said to have been the result of long bouts of head colds as a child. She was reportedly the least favored of the athletic, competitive Kelly siblings. It was in performing that she found her calling.

Jack and Margaret hoped she would outgrow her love of acting and perhaps settle down. By some accounts, Jack had looked down at the profession, allegedly seeing it as barely *"above streetwalker."* That fatherly approval never would come fully, even after all of Grace's successes. Some Hollywood pundits have even theorized that Grace Kelly's search for her father's approval led her to have romances with older men.

For Grace, the pull of performance and the arts remained strong in spite of her parent's lack of support. Ironically though, the arts were really in her blood and even in her name. She was named for her Aunt Grace, his father's sister, an actress who had died young. She had an uncle, Walter Kelly, who was an actor in vaudeville. Another uncle,

George Kelly, was a Pulitzer Prize-winning playwright.

After finishing high school, like many dreamers before her, Grace Kelly headed for the Big Apple. She enrolled at the American Academy of Dramatic Arts in 1947. Her parents were said to have wanted her to go to Bennington College, but her math skills were supposedly not up to par and she did not gain admission. Nevertheless, the Kellys did allow her New York move and schooling, but reportedly under the condition that she stayed at Manhattan's famous Barbizon Hotel.

Not just any hotel, the Barbizon was an institution, welcoming into its doors women with big dreams in the big city. It was like an incubator of female achievers, who could have some independence alongside a sense of safety (for some of the women, the rental bell still went to mommy and daddy even as they spread their wings pursuing careers as secretaries, models, actors, editors and other work in publishing – or finding a husband!). Some of the glitterati who 'graduated' from the single women's residence were Lauren Bacall, Joan Crawford, Candice Bergen, Cybill Shepherd, Joan Didion, Gene Tierney, Liza Minnelli and of course, Grace Kelly herself. Another of its famous residents, the iconic but ultimately tragic poet, Sylvia Plath, also called it home for a short time.

The Barbizon Hotel for Women stood at 23 stories high on the corner of East 63rd Street and Lexington Avenue in Manhattan. The 700-room hotel / dormitory was a fortress-like structure that opened in 1926 and indeed, approached the protection of the reputation of its young women with zeal. Applying for a spot could be tedious, and required multiple references, not to mention impeccable looks and demeanor. There were curfews and dress codes, and strict rules governing everything from food to the use of electrical appliances. Food was not allowed in the rooms and, just as prohibited were men. They were required to sign in upon entry and even then, were permitted only in a few public spaces; not that the spirited women of the Barbizon always followed this particular rule, for not a few of them have sneaked in the occasional guest.

It is delightful to imagine Grace Kelly in these gilded surroundings, cutting her teeth in New York in a prestigious address, amidst the energy of like-minded women. But even in a field of privilege, talent and ambition, someone always stands out from the rest and in many ways, Grace was among one of these. She was privileged, but she worked hard. And being a student at the American Academy of Dramatic Arts was tough. There was training for posture, manners, diction, pronunciation, control of movement, exercises for breathing, applying makeup, even walking and sitting down. The body was an instrument for communication.

While pursuing her craft, Grace Kelly also put her incredible looks to good use modeling, appearing in advertisements and on magazines. It supplemented her income, especially with limited financial support from her family. She was a pro, having been doing modeling since the age of 12.

Grace Kelly debuted on Broadway in 1949, for *The Father*. She was 19 years old. Her performance was found promising and fresh, and she was well-received not just by critics, but also by eagle-eyed television producers on the lookout for talent. The medium was on a post-war gold rush, and actresses for drama projects were in demand. Grace Kelly was beautiful, trained, professional, and had the grit for the demands of television. Over the early stages of her acting career, she would be credited in over 60 television dramas.

Though it was the stage that led her to the small screen, finding jobs on Broadway ultimately proved harder for her. It might have been her thin, nasal voice, which wasn't ideal for projecting in a theater. At least the stage led to small screen, and the small screen led her to the silver screen.

She acted in her first film, *Fourteen Hours* (1951) when she was 22. She had a minor role and was not particularly remarkable in it, especially by her own steep, artistic standards. She had a studio offer from her first Hollywood try, but the offer was not tempting enough for her to risk being typecast or limited. She decided to work on improving her acting instead, and returned to New York for further training and for the theater. She spent weeks in summer stock – theater productions in the professional off-season, held during the summer months – but Hollywood would soon come calling again.

Exactly how the newcomer got a plum part in *High Noon* (1952) is unclear, but by various reports, she was either approached by producer Stanley Kramer after seeing her in a production of *Elitch Gardens*; steered into the role by the famous actor Gary Cooper, who had seen something in her from her efforts in *Fourteen Hours*; or secured it after a meeting with director Fred Zinnemann; or perhaps all of the above. Either way, she secured the role of Amy Kane for *High Noon*. It wasn't just a minor role, either. She was going to play the veteran actor's wife and – spoiler alert! – buck against expectations and help save the day.

In the well-received Western, Grace Kelly played the tough town Marshal's young, new Quaker bride. She had a kind of posh, wooden, misplacedness that fit the role of a pacifist wife in the Wild West. The film would win Gary Cooper the Academy Award for Best Actor, but he was admirable in other ways. He was 28 years Kelly's senior, and he reportedly took the time to coach her. For Grace Kelly, though, it wasn't just a learning experience. Starring in *High Noon* brought her to the big leagues. It was just her second film, but she was already part of a movie that rapidly became a classic.

Soon, she was on a film set with established talent for Academy Award-winning director, John Ford's *Mogambo* (1953). As Linda Nordley, she is the fish-out-of-water in Kenya, vying for Clark Gable's big-game hunter against sultry socialite Ava Gardner. It was an important time in her career. She had landed a seven-year contract. For *Mogambo*, she would be nominated at the

Oscars for the first time, in the Supporting Actress category. She would also win a Best Supporting Actress nod from the Golden Globes. Grace Kelly was relatively new in Hollywood, but was quickly becoming known not only as a fine young beauty with elegance and poise, but also as an actress with a good grasp of her craft.

The acting accolades for *Mogambo* were reportedly a surprise for the actress, however. The self-critique is not new; in *High Noon*, she was reportedly dissatisfied with her performance and wanted to be better. She was always serious about performance, and never afraid of doing hard work. She would even insist on caveats within her MGM contract, to limit the number of pictures she made in a year so that she could also spend time in New York and hone her craft on stage. She was also protective of her image and the roles she played. Among her quirks were her general displeasure over publicity, her refusal to reveal her vital statistics (at the time, it was normal to do so), refusal to suffer an invasive makeover, and refusal to appear in B-movies. Even heavy makeup was a no-no. For example, in *To Catch a Thief*, she reportedly used no foundation, and could have makeup done in as little as seven minutes.

Over the course of her career, she stuck to her guns and showed willingness to suffer suspension to get her way. In days when the studios were the undisputed kings of Hollywood, the stars might have been packaged in wealth and glamour but they actually had very limited power in their creative lives. Many contracts bound talent to projects designed around the studios' goals for them. Refusal often meant not only no pay, but also no permission to work anywhere else. Suspension had very real consequences for the present and future income of an artist.

At the time it was practically unheard of in Hollywood, for a young, relatively new actress to not only have a desire to determine her own creative fate, but also to have the courage to assert herself and be willing to lose opportunities, as well as risk her boss' ire or her income. But Grace Kelly, by the time she arrived in Tinsel Town, was already her own woman. From her modeling work, she knew how she wanted to look, and what looked good on her. She was also financially secure from her family wealth as well as her own work outside of the movies, and she did not need much money because she did not indulge in a lavish lifestyle in the first place. She was actually reportedly rather frugal – a trait she would always carry, as she was fond of reusing her wardrobe. She was also well-educated and well-raised. Thus, she had the privilege to say no to roles she did not like - an option she would exercise several times in her career. Her financial standing and courage allowed her to be selective with parts, and she would actually risk suspension for the role that would get her an Academy Award win for Best Actress in a Leading Role, for *The Country Girl* (1954).

As her star rose, Grace Kelly had a selection of offers, and would even turn down *On the Waterfront* (1954) with Marlon Brando. The role she had passed on, that of Edie Doyle, would secure the actress Eva Marie Saint an

Academy Award for Best Supporting Actress in 1955 – not that Grace Kelly had too much room for regret. That was the year she won the Oscar for her lead role in *The Country Girl*. She starred with established actors, Bing Crosby and William Holden, and played against type as an alcoholic has-been actor's drab wife. To secure the win, Kelly had to best trailblazing Dorothy Dandridge in *Carmen Jones*, iconic Judy Garland in *A Star Is Born*, and previous Oscar winners, Jane Wyman in *Magnificent Obsession*, and Audrey Hepburn in *Sabrina*.

She cemented her talent in *The Country Girl*, but Grace Kelly would best be remembered in her ice queen glory. And this image was best executed whenever she was in the creative path of suspense genius Alfred Hitchcock, for a string of critically-acclaimed and commercially-successful films, *Dial M for Murder* (1954), *Rear Window* (1954), and *To Catch a Thief* (1955).

Hollywood's Ice Queen

Alfred Hitchcock was once quoted as saying, *"It is ice that will burn your hands."*

The director had a well-deserved reputation as Hollywood's 'Master of Suspense.' He was known for his work in bold, thought-provoking movies with powerful, unforgettable imagery. He had a soft spot for a complex, icy blond hiding secrets and passions beneath her cool, aloof exterior – and Grace Kelly could have been born to work with him. Of the actress, he had once said that her frigidity was akin to "...*a mountain covered with snow, but that mountain was a volcano...*" In Alfred Hitchcock's hands, her icy sophistication was not brittle, but a powerful veneer. It wasn't shallow aloofness, it was deep restraint, and the filmmaker thrilled audiences with unfurling her complex layers.

In *Dial M for Murder*, she is Margot Wendice, adulterous wife to murderous husband, Tony Wendice (played by Oscar winner, Ray Milland). Tony is the frustrated mastermind trying to arrange his wealthy wife's death to get her money, but the hardier-than-expected Margot proves easier to frame for murder than to actually murder. In *Rear Window*, she plays socialite and all-around perfect girl, Lisa Carol Fremont opposite (another Oscar winning actor) James Stewart's wheelchair-bound ace photographer, L.B. Jeffries. L.B.'s temporary disability has him obsessed with watching his neighbors from his apartment window, and is soon convinced there is foul play going on between a husband and wife across the street. Lisa does the legwork as his surprisingly courageous and adventurous partner in solving the crime. In *To Catch a Thief*, Grace Kelly's final film with Hitchcock, she stars opposite Cary Grant's reformed cat burglar, John Robie, as the privileged Frances Stevens. Frances and her mother, a wealthy widow, become the target of a Robie copycat while vacationing in the French Riviera. Sparks fly between Robie and the perceptive, seductive Frances – until the Stevens' jewels are lost and suspicions fall on Robie.

Grace Kelly was luminous and unforgettable in all these films, Hitchcock adored having her in them, and the work arrangements also worked out for her studio, MGM. They were making money loaning her talents out to the filmmaker. Indeed, the collaboration seemed favorable to all parties. For Grace, working with Hitchcock allowed her some leeway against simply giving in to her contractual obligations of accepting any and all studio-assigned parts. As for what Hitchcock saw...

Around the time he was casting for *Dial M...*, Hitchcock screened *Mogambo* but was reportedly unimpressed by Grace Kelly, especially by her voice. But he did look at Kelly's *Taxi* screen test (a part she lost to actress Constance Smith), and was intrigued enough to want to meet with her. He saw for himself her dreamy blond beauty but also her restraint and underlying sexual allure. He saw a kind of duality in her that would be cultivated in *Dial M...*, as she played prim wife one moment, sensual adulteress in the next.

Alfred Hitchcock could be overwhelming for his leading ladies (some say, even abusive), but he and Grace worked well together. He had patience with the actress, and she was willing to learn from him. They also shared a sense of humor. Creatively, Hitchcock and Kelly both carried a theater approach into their film work. *Dial M…*, after all, had been a play acquired by Hitchcock for film, and he very much intended to bring in that same constrained quality into his movie. It was in a sense, a filmed play – which likely resonated with an actress like Grace Kelly, who held theater in high regard. Her dramatic training came in handy too, as *Dial M…* had her acting with her whole body, with some scenes not even showing her face.

Hitchcock found himself a muse, and reportedly had Grace early in his sights for his next project, even before production for *Dial M…* was finished. This next project was *Rear Window*, and Grace would reportedly pass on *On the Waterfront* with Marlon Brando to work with Hitchcock again.

Rear Window is based on a short story by Cornell Woolrich, which then initially came into the hands of Joshua Logan, before being firmly held by radio writer John Michael Hayes as scriptwriter. Grace Kelly's Lisa was an addition to the original, and the character was basically designed around her. Hitchcock had even arranged for Hayes to spend time with Kelly and include some of her traits in the writing. The result was a character who had some of Grace Kelly's true self in it, and some of Hayes' wife, who was also a former model. And so in Lisa Carol Fremont, it's as if we see Grace Kelly herself unfurl; a lively girl of warmth and humor beneath an icy, sophisticated, oh-so-perfect (perhaps too perfect) façade.

Next on the pipeline for the formidable pair was *To Catch a Thief*, based on a novel by David Dodge. Again, Hitchcock had Grace Kelly in mind early on – a choice shared by the movie's principal actor, Cary Grant, who was open in his admiration of her skill and control as an actress. MGM loaned her to Hitchcock and Paramount for the project (getting something in exchange of course, in this case, the talents of hot actor William Holden). The film is lighter than the usual Hitchcock fare, a charming, breezy production filmed for the most part, on location in the South of France. Grace Kelly was, as usual, exquisite in her ice cold glory and subtly unfolding, well-paced, surprising sexiness. She was classy but sensual, bright and funny – some would say, simply perfect. The ideal woman.

Well-received though it was, *To Catch a Thief* was the last of their projects together, and Hitchcock would seek his ideal, icy femme fatale elsewhere afterwards. The director liked having complex blondes in his films for a miscellany of declared and theorized reasons, among them that (1) they photographed well in black and white; (2) that gradual breaking of their cool veneer as a character becomes more articulated, tended to up the surprise factor in a movie; and (3) they represented perfect women he could completely control where he otherwise would not have been able to attain them. The last is a theory that is inspired by his overbearing, controlling, almost obsessive approach upon the actresses on his films. With Grace Kelly though, he was said to have been mostly a gentleman, and had even been willing to listen to her input. This was a rarity, especially as it required the director to make adjustments from his meticulously-set scenes to adhere to her suggestions.

After Hitchcock's three-picture collaboration with Grace Kelly, he tried to capture that same magic with the archetype that would eventually be known as The Hitchcock Blonde – characters that are complex, mysterious, perhaps a little duplicitous, who were played by an icy, stunning blond actress. Among them were Kim Novak in *Vertigo* (1958); Eva Marie Saint in *North by Northwest* (1959); Janet Leigh in *Psycho* (1960); and Tippi Hedren in *The Birds* (1963) and *Marnie* (1964).

How Grace Kelly could have embodied iconic roles like these in such unforgettable movies, we will never know... for she would leave Hollywood all too soon to play the biggest part of her life. That of Princess Grace of Monaco.

A Reel and Real Femme Fatale

Younger generations would know Grace Kelly best for her glamorous, royal persona. She was that unflappable blond who captured audiences in Hollywood and turned away from Tinsel Town to win the heart of a real prince. She even looked as if she was born to be a princess.

The sad truth is that many beautiful women come and go in Hollywood, and even those who have accolades and talent to match their beauty do not always have enduring relevance or continuing cultural impact. In short - beauty and talent just aren't enough to create a legend. In the case of Grace Kelly though, her status as Hollywood legend is, ironically because first, she was willing to leave it behind. It wasn't just about leaving it *at her prime* to become a princess, note – she had always showed courage in risking opportunities and income in pursuit of a worthy and challenging part. Second, in a land of naked opportunists and publicity-hungry performers, she always showed a preference for keeping many aspects of her life private. Like the roles that would define her, she had control and restraint… and she also had complexity and secrets.

Grace Kelly won audiences with her icy beauty and red hot talent. She'd won over her directors and her co-stars too, who praised her humor, hard work, professionalism and thoroughness. But in her private life, she would also win over a collection of lovers. She had so many real and rumored conquests, that tales of wild, romantic exploits would spread about her, including allegations of nymphomania. In her beautiful, swanlike wake, she may have left behind broken hearts and broken marriages.

The rogue's gallery of Kelly's alleged lovers gives passing mention to her early conquests when she was a young woman finding her way in New York. Here, it is said that she dated fellow young actors and classmates. But one of the most controversial figures in her dating history was acting instructor, Don Richardson.

He was only 28 when they were in each other's lives, but Don Richardson would go on to have a long and respectable career in the arts. When he passed away in 1996, he left behind 50 years of work as an acting teacher and as a director on Broadway and television. He also wrote a book, *Acting Without Agony: An Alternative to the Method*, that is used all over the world. Over his years as an instructor, he counted among his students the likes of Anne Bancroft, Elizabeth Montgomery, Zero Mostel and, famously Grace Kelly. She was only 17 years old when she came into the American Academy of Dramatic Arts in New York.

Some have credited Richardson for the making of Grace Kelly as she is known; though this feat, of course, could also be said of her Pulitzer Prize-winning Uncle George

Kelly who nurtured her love of the arts and whose name supposedly got her foot in the door. It could also be said of director Alfred Hitchcock, who taught her about filmmaking and captured her most iconic images. It could even be said of designer and eventual boyfriend Oleg Cassini, who had helped style her. Grace Kelly is clearly an agglomeration of what is desirable to many men, who may have each had a contribution in the graceful final product. For his part, Richardson is reputed to have influenced Grace Kelly in important ways in her student years in New York. They dated for a few years after all, with a large gap in their age and experience. He was also, at the end of the day, an educator. It makes sense that he would have had some expertise to share.

Richardson is said to have helped her by securing her first agent, and by helping her get her first Broadway role in *The Father*. He may have also been the one to steer her away from her Philadelphia accent. It is unverified how far his influence went or how much of a Pygmalion he was to the early incarnation of Grace Kelly, but what is certain is that Richardson recognized her ambition, and always thought she showed promise of stardom.

Their affair, however, had a much bleaker future than her acting career. When she brought him to Philadelphia to meet her family, he was practically turned out. Her father, the already-impossible to please John Kelly, allegedly had an anti-Semitic streak to boot, which did not bode well for Richardson even before the family's distressful discovery of his still-upcoming divorce. If rumors hold true, Richardson would eventually even be offered a luxury vehicle by the older Kellys - a Jaguar! - if he would just leave Grace alone. It was declined, but the relationship would nevertheless still end.

Some say Grace Kelly had only used Richardson only as a stepping stone to feed her hungry ambition. Then again, some people also said she liked dancing nude to Hawaiian music, and other stories would have her dancing in her underwear at the halls of the legendary Barbizon Hotel. Another tale has her modeling lingerie in New York, and popping by a lover's apartment during break time. And did she really romance the Waldorf Astoria's maître d'? The goal, allegedly being that of finding opportunities to connect with influential men who could boost her career. If the hotel maître d' wasn't spared her charms, it should come as no surprise that she was also allegedly able to romance married men. If you looked at source after source speculating on Grace Kelly's alleged love affairs, they read just like her resume. Could she really have romanced so many of the men she co-starred with?

She starred in *High Noon* with actor Gary Cooper and director Fred Zinnermann; rumors are that she ended up romancing them both. Cooper, at the time, was reportedly married but separated and in a relationship with another actress, Patricia Neal. But he did fit into the mold that was allegedly Grace Kelly's romantic weakness;

he was much older (28 years her senior) and somewhat of a fatherly figure.

Next she was in *Mogambo* with Clark Gable (who is also 28 years older than she). Grace Kelly has been quoted as saying something to the effect of, 'what else was there to do in a tent in Africa with Clark Gable?' But is the quote accurate and even if it were, was she being serious considering she had a wicked, mischievous sense of humor? And if the answer to these questions are yes, how far into the off-screen did they really take their onscreen romance?

In *Dial M for Murder*, director Alfred Hitchcock reportedly had an unhealthy infatuation for her, but it is not known if and how she may have encouraged it, or if she reciprocated in any way. But that is only just one of the rumors about Kelly's romantic and / or sexual entanglements in this film. Her co-star, Oscar winner, Ray Milland (24 years her senior), is said to have fallen deeply in love with her and she, with him. The snag? He's long been married to Muriel Weber, and they had children together. But did his wife Muriel really kick him out? And did Kelly and Milland live together in a shared apartment and considered getting married, as has been suggested by gossip? Did Kelly deserve the antagonistic wave in the Hollywood community that followed these rumors, and to be called a homewrecker for it? Did her actions really merit gossip columnist and entertainment icon, Hedda Hopper's label of a nymphomaniac?

Grace was reportedly shocked and unprepared for the vitriol against her following the Milland situation. Hollywood pundits would later note that she had 'a healthy sexual appetite,' and was not a promiscuous type; she really seemed to be looking for affection, approval and love. The antagonism probably stemmed from the wide disparity between the image she projected, as best symbolized by her fancy white gloves, with her scandalous private life.

Unfortunately after all that grief, Milland still wasn't The One. Either by Kelly family interference, or Milland's lingering affection for his wife, or Milland's realization of the ghastly financial impact a divorce would have on him (with properties apparently made out in Muriel's name!), or a combination of all three, the romance fizzled out. Milland went back to his wife and would be with her until his death in 1986, while Grace Kelly sashayed her way into another controversial romantic dalliance.

Hollywood playboy, William Holden (11 years older than the actress), would also have a shot with the ice queen, for he starred with Grace Kelly in both *The Bridges at Toko-Ri* (1954) and *The Country Girl*. At the time, Holden was married to his long-suffering wife, actress Brenda "Ardis" Marshall, who was reportedly aware of her husband's indiscretions. Holden and Kelly allegedly had a steamy affair, cut short only because he had previously had a vasectomy. Interestingly enough, a similar rumor follows William Holden and actress Audrey Hepburn, with whom he starred in *Sabrina*

(1954); co-stars madly in love, Holden willing to leave his wife, a break-up after his vasectomy is discovered... which shows that perhaps, rumors are really rather difficult to believe. Perhaps Grace Kelly was, as some sources note, just on the rebound from Ray Milland.

Another theory is that Holden and Kelly's romance ended because of Bing Crosby. The three were co-stars in *The Country Girl*, and Crosby and Kelly got along swimmingly even if Crosby did not originally want Grace Kelly for the role of his wife. He thought she was too beautiful and was skeptical her acting abilities could handle the heavyweight part (of course, she would end up winning an Academy Award for it). Holden, if rumors are true, may have stepped down for Crosby, who was a massive crossover superstar. Crosby, a recent widower, was in high demand in film, music, and radio. He was an Oscar winner and a chart-topper, with more hits than The Beatles or Elvis. Holden may have backed away to avoid a collision he likely would have lost if Crosby decided to push his considerable weight.

Not that the Crosby-Kelly romance had much steam. Their romance would end, allegedly due to Marlon Brando; though rumors of Crosby catching them in bed after the Academy Awards (in which Kelly won for *The Country Girl* and Brando took home the Best Actor trophy for *On the Waterfront*), just seems too unlikely. Kelly and Crosby worked together again in her last film before she left Hollywood behind though – *High Society* (1956). They settled with being close friends, and he would even help her land a hit song, via their duet, the soundtrack *True Love*. Another cast member, however, would allegedly capture Grace's attention – she may have explored a relationship with Frank Sinatra, too.

Non-actors would make it to Grace Kelly's hit list, via the successful designer, Oleg Cassini. Cassini had been hit hard by Kelly-fever after *Mogambo*, and he was determined to have her. He reportedly even sent her roses every day until she agreed to a meal with him. He was doing well in his field (and would famously dress First Lady of the United States and style icon, Jackie Kennedy), and came from a line of Russian aristocrats. He had a hand in her styling, adding some sexuality to her look. Grace was reportedly interested in marrying him (he later said they were in love and engaged). His romantic history, however, was less than impressive to the Kelly matriarch, what with divorces and children. Though he was technically free to have a relationship with Grace Kelly, innuendo wouldn't escape this pair either, and rumors of pregnancy and abortion would be linked to them.

Royalty also wouldn't escape a Grace Kelly connection, even before Prince Rainier III of Monaco swept her away to his principality. The Shah of Iran might have been a suitor, as well as Prince Aly Kahn. American political royalty may have also been in the actress' sphere, as she was rumored to have dated John F. Kennedy.

Other men would be connected to Grace Kelly aside from these; photos of the actress with French actor Jean-Pierre Aumont would come out in the tabloids too, and actor David Niven once recalled almost saying "Grace Kelly" when asked by Prince Rainier about exciting lovers. A few other names would pop up in rumor and innuendo – Richard Boccelli, Tony Curtis, Cary Grant, Anthony Havelock-Allan, Gene Lyons, James Stewart, Sidney Wood… and these are only the prominent men. There were allegedly unknown others.

So with this rather lengthy list of alleged conquests, was Grace Kelly a misunderstood flirt or some sort of a sex addict? Was she really looking for the love of a father figure in every man? Who in her list of alleged conquests are true and who are false and to what extent? Was she looking for sex or romance? Was she naïve or promiscuous? She definitely had mystique, and the racy stories about her sometimes border on the fantastic and unbelievable. Could these crazy rumors even be just a little bit true? Or has she perhaps captured everyone in a collective fantasy of imagining the prim, glacial blond in the most unlikely of sexual scenarios?

Was there really a simmering siren underneath all that ice?

She had ensnared legendary Alfred Hitchcock in that irresistible duality, and he in turn had helped perpetuate that fantasy via unforgettable movie magic. It seems then, that the public can never truly know 'the real' Grace Kelly under all that ice.

Letters written by Grace Kelly to her personal secretary and good friend, Prudence Wise, would be made available at auction a few years after her death. The correspondence spanned two decades, covering some of Grace Kelly's most exciting periods in Hollywood. They were pretty candid, and discussed her co-stars and alleged lovers in warm, friendly terms. When asked, a representative from the owner of the collection said that there seemed to be no hints of romance with anyone other than Clark Gable. Could it be then, that all of these affairs are really unsubstantiated, or did she just not confide about them?

The actress was never afraid of keeping some things to herself and there are many secrets she would take to the grave. In addressing some of the rumors about her, she'd simply said in general terms, that as an unmarried women, she was perceived as a threat. Whether or not that threat was actualized and with whom, we might never know. That sense of mystery, that tease, is part of her enduring appeal.

Princess Grace of Monaco

In the mid-1950s, Grace Kelly was at a turning point in her life.

She didn't know it yet, but she had already made most of the movies that would make up her filmography: her 1951 debut, *Fourteen Hours*; her instant Western classic, *High Noon* in 1952; her critically acclaimed acting performance for *Mogambo* in 1953; her Oscar winning turn in *The Country Girl* (1954); her iconic icy moments as Alfred Hitchcock's muse in *Dial M for Murder* (1954), *Rear Window* (1954), and *To Catch a Thief* (1955); and the average *Green Fire* (1954) and *The Bridges at Toko-Ri* (1954). She found that her Academy Award win didn't quite lead to parts that compelled her, and she was also dissatisfied with her personal life while her sisters were well-settled with families of their own.

It was at these professional and personal crossroads that she would meet Prince Charming.

A Royal Romance

The romance between Grace Kelly and her Prince had a glamorous start. The setting? It was 1955, and Grace was in France for the Cannes Film Festival as part of the American delegation. Oscar winning actress Olivia de Havilland and her new husband, *Paris-Match* editor Pierre Galante, convinced Grace to visit Monaco for an audience and photo session with Prince Rainer III.

Fate was feeling a little mischievous that day, and Grace was beset by small inconveniences on her way to her date with destiny. Her hotel suffered in an electricity strike, which prevented her from preparing properly. Instead of a hair dryer, she had to settle for a floral headband. Instead of a pressed attire, she had to settle for a dress she was not confident in. There was a fender-bender. The Prince himself arrived late, nearly missing the Hollywood superstar.

But meet they did, and the rest is history...

... or, not quite. For complex and compelling public figures, love and marriage can never be quite so straightforward. Prince Rainier, born on the 31st of May, 1923, had been sitting on the throne since the age of 26. He was 32 when he met Grace Kelly and eager for a bride. Over the years, he was said to be aware of the increasing need to start a family and produce an heir, which was necessary for Monaco to continue to be independent. For a long time, he had been in a relationship with actress Gisele Pascal, but he had big ambitions that did not quite have a place for her. They broke up and she married and started a family with another actor. Rainier, on the other hand, started nurturing his big dreams for Monaco and navigating how to get there with the perfect Princess.

The Catholic Rainier had an unexpected matchmaker on his side. His spiritual advisor, Father Tucker, looked into the possibilities of the Prince's union with other Catholic girls, including Grace Kelly. She was beautiful, accomplished, classy, and like Rainier, raised devout. It certainly helped that their first meeting left them both intrigued by the other, and they managed to keep a lively correspondence even when she left and returned to the United States. It was also somewhat fortuitous that Grace Kelly's next movie was *The Swan* (1956) – where she played a Princess.

Later that year, Prince Rainier visited the United States for a diplomatic tour… and a proposal! Monaco wasn't very well-known in the country at the time, but the impossible-to-impress Jack and Margaret Kelly suddenly had a titled aristocrat from an old European family asking for their daughter's hand in marriage, and probably for the first time, they were ready to approve of their middle daughter's life choices. Even her Oscar for *The Country Girl* had proved not particularly moving for them, but Prince Rainier III and what he could do for the family's standing in Philadelphia was definitely something the Kelly couple could be proud of. But before anything else, Grace Kelly reportedly had to be checked for fertility, and the matter of her infamous $2 million dowry (to cover part of the wedding costs had to be resolved. Good thing Jack Kelly was a multi-millionaire and wanted his daughter to be a princess.

There was also the issue of her career – Rainier found it improper for his royal bride to continue to be in the movies and as a matter of fact, Grace Kelly's films would eventually be banned in Monaco. But Grace moved forward with the union, reportedly in the hopes that she might one day be able to change his mind.

Soon enough, all signs were pointing go, even if the couple had not known each other for very long. Maybe she married the Prince to please her father. Maybe she went through with it because she didn't know she could never return to acting. As for Rainier, maybe he was in a rush to marry the paper and picture perfect bride to be his Princess and make an heir. Maybe he saw the perfect complement for his dreams for his country. Then again, maybe they really were madly in love.

Either way – being Princess of Monaco brought Grace Kelly into her Third Act. She'd already leapt from stage and television to the giant, intimidating sea of Hollywood. Now she was on the curious intersection between politics and entertainment. She was entering the world of old world royalty.

A public announcement of the engagement was made in the Kelly's stately Philadelphia home. And that staple of royal romances everywhere, a breathtaking engagement ring, was featured on the beautiful bride-to-be's famously elegant and expressive hand. The ring is a huge 10.47-carat, emerald-cut diamond on a platinum band. It stars alongside Kelly in her las feature film, *High Society*, where it catches the audience's attention as Bing Crosby's character famously remarks, "*Some stone, did you mine it yourself?*"

Grace Kelly capped off her Hollywood career by playing socialite Tracy Lord in *High Society*, and then she was off to Monaco with her family for the so-called 'wedding of the century.' Her mother Margaret Kelly was reportedly disappointed that the ceremony, held on the 19th of April, 1956, wouldn't be before the family's peers (and snobbish critics!) in Philadelphia. It may have comforted her to know that few in America could have missed it. MGM, which proved amenable to their star's early Hollywood exit especially since they were getting exclusive rights to film her wedding, would make footage accessible to a wide audience. There were 600 guests at the event, but a whole lot more people lined the streets to cheer the couple (20,000 by some estimates), and even more were able to catch it on television; *The Wedding in Monaco* captured a 30 million-strong TV audience when it aired. The studio was also generous to their star, and sent her off with a bonus, her character Tracy Lord's *High Society* wardrobe, and the unforgettable

Helen Rose creation that would make wedding history.

Long after the wedding, the gown designed by MGM's wardrobe wizard spent some time in the Philadelphia Museum of Art, and it was a much deserved place. It really is a piece of art, this $8,000 silk taffeta dress with antique rose-point lace and pearls, which took three dozen seamstresses, six weeks to make. It was well worth the effort and attention; ever since Grace walked down the aisle in it, it has become *the* wedding gown to judge all royal wedding gowns to come after it, including the recent breathtaking, Sarah Burton for Alexander McQueen piece worn by Catherine Middleton, when she married Prince William in England in 2011.

Royal on the Rise

By her marriage to Rainier, Grace had acquired a multitude of titles aside from "Princess of Monaco." She was Princess Chateau-Porciean too, and several times over each: a duchess, a countess, a marquise, and a baroness. She had joined an esteemed line of aristocrats. Her husband's family, the Grimaldis, is among the oldest ruling European families, and have been connected to Monaco since 1297.

Her new home is the world's second smallest country, undersized only by the Vatican. It is so small that the land area is about the size of Central Park in Manhattan. One of the biggest attractions here is the Casino Monte Carlo, which actually bars Monegasque citizens, for gambling is illegal to them.

Gambling revenues from visiting foreigners is limited, accounting for a small percentage of the economy. A larger chunk comes from tourism and why shouldn't it? Tourists may want to see the principality for themselves, what with cinematic icons like Iron Man (in *Iron Man 3*) and James Bond visiting often (in *Never Say Never* Again, *Golden Eye* and *Casino Royale*) onscreen. Monaco does not collect income taxes and has a reputation for being a tax haven. Its citizens enjoy a high standard of living, and many millionaires and billionaires either call it home, or use it as a playground – among them, Bono and George Clooney. Some of its most glamorous events are the Monaco Grand Prix, and the Monaco Yacht Show.

It wasn't always this way. Though the tiny country was beautiful and the Grimaldi family ruling it was well-established, the postwar economics were not very sound. When Prince Rainier came to the throne in 1949, the aging casinos, hotels and tourist attractions were experiencing staggering losses. Competition with other locales for gambling and tourism was fierce. In the first years of the 1950s, the Societe Monegasque de Banques et de Metaux Precieux, went bankrupt. Monaco seemed to need an invigorating shot in the arm.

According to legend, Greek magnate Aristotle Onassis conceived of the idea that Monaco's Prince Rainier III should marry a superstar, and put the country back on the map. If that's not even more fantastic, the suggested star had been no one less than Marilyn Monroe (who was reportedly not inclined to cooperate). Whether or not this is true or if the Prince Rainier had even known about it, is uncertain. Either way, whether or not by design, the desired effect was accomplished by Rainier's marriage to Grace Kelly, which did have an important impact on the country.

The 'wedding of the century' certainly increased tourism revenues. But she also gave Monaco recall and prestige, and indirectly, helped increase flows of capital into the country which in turn, stimulated it to modernize, attract other investments, and decrease its reliance on gambling income. With Grace's ambassadorial image and Rainier's daring vision, Monaco's economy became more diverse and it flourished for a long time. The government coffers had funds, even social security made money, and unemployment was stunningly low.

It is hard to imagine a setting and lifestyle more fitting to someone of Grace Kelly's wealth, style and elegance. It certainly seemed like an ideal home for a 26-year-old American Princess. But at the beginning, it wasn't the case at all. Grace reportedly did not connect very well with the Grimaldis, save perhaps for her husband's father, Prince Pierre. Rainier's mother, Princess Charlotte, as well as his sister, Princess Antoinette, were said to be more lukewarm in their reception of the actress. Grace also found life in her new home difficult. Before becoming its ruler's wife, she had only visited once after all. She knew some of French but the language and accent in Monaco proved challenging to her. She also suffered from depression after giving birth, and after having miscarriages. Her father Jack's death in 1960 also compounded her tumultuous feelings at the early period of her marriage.

Prince Rainier tried his best to help his wife, and though he had banned her films in his country after they were married, he was reportedly initially supportive of her return to the screen. She was, after all, an artist. She was proud of her work, and it couldn't have been easy turning away from the passion for performance that she's had and fought for since she was a child. That she had to leave acting behind was probably one of her few regrets.

The question was, however, what would be a comeback worthy of her Serene Highness, the Princess of Monaco? Even after years away from the movies, Grace Kelly could still have had her pick of parts. But there was one man who had an edge above the competition – visionary filmmaker, the Master of Suspense himself, Alfred Hitchcock.

Hitchcock adored his seminal icy blond, and even pursued her after her royal retirement – discreetly, of course, out of deference to her new status as a princess. He had purchased rights to bring to life the Winston Graham novel *Marnie* (1964) on film, but could not find the right actress. He eventually imagined it to be Grace Kelly's comeback film, and went through her agents for them to pass it on to her. Hitchcock claimed never to have broached the topic directly to Kelly, even if he did see her and her husband several times while in France. The princess not only agreed to do it, it had even been announced by a Monaco palace official in 1962.

Unfortunately, she would eventually withdraw. The official reason was scheduling conflict... but there could have been many other possible obstructions to her return to the big screens. First, there was some confusion on her contractual obligations with MGM – was her relationship with them terminated or merely suspended when she retired from acting in 1956? Were they, therefore, entitled to demand participation in Hitchcock's project? Second, there was also a question of the Princess' salary – how much would it be, and / or would there be a share of the profits? The question of money ushered in an entirely new issue all on its own – was Monaco in financial straits, such that the

Princess needed to return to filmmaking to help them along? This last one had to be addressed decisively, and Rainier and Grace would say that the film project coincided with Grace's plans to spend time with her family in America. Furthermore, they claimed the funds would be used for charity.

Not to be left out of consideration were the opinions of the press and the people. There wasn't just speculation on why Princess Grace was returning to work, there was also criticism of it. Apparently, the citizens of Monaco had qualms about their princess playing a woman of questionable morals on screen. There may have also been pressure from her husband and / or France's Charles de Gaulle and / or conservative and powerful voices in Monaco, against her return to film in this incarnation, or in any incarnation. The timing may have actually been bad too, either way – Hitchcock postponed work on *Marnie* due to the small gap between its start and the completion of Hitchcock's work on *The Birds*, which could have steered the schedule away from Grace's family visit to America. Politics may have also played a part – around that time, France was exerting pressure on Monaco regarding its tax system, and was holding over its head the conclusion of a treaty that would have affected such pivotal things as water and electric supply if it was not re-negotiated. Rainier, therefore, could not leave until the matter was settled and neither could his wife.

For whatever reason then, whether or not it was from a single cause or a confluence of events, Princess Grace bowed out of *Marnie* and the role eventually went to Tippi Hedren, another icy blond who had worked with Alfred Hitchcock previously on *The Birds* (1963).

The *Marnie* fallout pretty much cemented how far removed Grace Kelly had become, from the possibility of ever returning to her old life as an actress. She reportedly pondered and privately lamented the roles she could have played and the great movies she could have made, but she made do and moved on. She devoted her time in Monaco to her role as Princess, and it was very much a role indeed, for she would employ the same techniques that she did in her craft in its execution. She researched the part, modified her behavior, and became very much the conservative royal.

Perhaps her legendary film collaborator, Alfred Hitchcock really did understand her well because when he was first asked to react to news of her engagement, he expressed happiness that Grace Kelly had secured *"such a good part."*

She approached royalty like acting work, and Grace Kelly always was very hard working and professional. According to reports, a typical day for the Princess would start as early as 7:15 AM, spent on her desk for several hours before she received guests and visitors at the palace. The rest of the day was spent making or listening to presentations, and appearances at benefits and galas for a miscellany of charities and projects. Her charitable endeavors included heading the Monaco Red Cross, founding AMADE Mondiale (a charitable organization focusing on the needs and rights of children all over the world), and advocating for special needs in Monaco. She also found a way to infuse her love of the arts with her role as a Princess; she helped protect and preserve historic structures, and became a patron of the arts. Her projects included festivals and fundraisers that are still running up to now.

She accomplished many things, even while she coped with difficulties in her home life. She and her Prince Charming would actually eventually spend much of their latter years apart. There were rumors of marital tension and affairs, though many in their inner circle would say they had a relatively solid partnership.

The children were also somewhat problematic. Their eldest, Princess Caroline, married a French playboy in 1978 and divorced him in 1980. Her romantic troubles would keep her father's hands full even after Grace passed away with a marriage that ended in a tragic accident, and her current, troubled one with Prince Ernst August of Hanover. Stephanie also proved difficult after Grace's tragic death, with controversial and short-lived romances featuring her bodyguard, an elephant trainer, and an acrobat. Prince Albert, who would succeed his father in 2005, also has his own woes, which includes illegitimate children and rumors of his bride trying to run away. As of this writing though, they are still together and have young twins.

Legacy

Can you really be a Hollywood legend, when your film career is basically comprised of a few good years and barely a dozen films? Where many of them are in the supporting role? Where the role that got you an Academy Award is actually how you are least remembered? Where you retired from the movies at age 26? It was a film career cut short no matter which way you look at it – as high as its trajectory it might have been, as magically as it might have ended.

It wasn't just her Hollywood career that would come to an abrupt halt. Grace Kelly, at the age of just 52, passed away in 1982 when she suffered a stroke while driving a car in Monaco. Her daughter Stephanie was with her when their car swerved off a treacherous coastal road and slid down the mountainside. Stephanie was hurt but not too seriously. Grace, on the other hand, would never regain consciousness and died soon afterwards. Her very life was cut tragically short.

And yet with these short years she still remains one of the most interesting public figures to have ever walked the Earth. Tributes to Grace Kelly can be found across continents. There is of course, the coveted Hermes Kelly bag, once known as the Haut a Courroie, renamed for the woman who was popularly seen and photographed with the iconic purse, especially as she used it to hide her baby bump from the press. In the United States, she was the first actress on a postage stamp, issued in 1993. In 2007, two-euro commemorative coins featured her profile.

And in a move that might finally have pleased her father, Jack B. Kelly, the Henley Royal Regatta, an esteemed rowing event, renamed a women's race after her – The Princess Grace Challenge Cup. She is widely considered to be one of the greatest female stars of all time, including by the American Film Institute. Her memorabilia continues to attract vast sums at auctions, and every once in a while, a fresh new facet of her personality comes out, capturing our attention again. In that gradual, carefully controlled and restrained Grace Kelly way – she unfurls again, showing us more of herself through recovered letters, collectibles and accounts of friends.

It has been revealed that she remained very down to earth, and had a pragmatic mind. She valued her family and her past, and would even return constantly to Philadelphia visiting the St. Bridget Catholic Church where she was baptized and where her family worshipped. She had a famous sense of humor and was known to indulge in a bawdy joke or a hearty laugh. Just as in her Hollywood career, she was not comfortable wearing heavy makeup in her daily life. One of the world's most stylish women not only when she was alive but up to the present, was actually not often in designer clothes. She was comfortable wearing simple pieces by the local seamstresses of Monaco, and famously reused clothes, sometimes for years on end. They could be anything from a beloved coat, to her maternity wear and yes, even the dress she won her Academy Award in. She loved games like charades, and had a passion for astrology. She kept her hands busy with handicrafts like knitting, crochet and pottery, and she loved tooling around in the soil, for she had a passion for gardening. The world often saw her and currently remembers her for her white gloves, but her hands have also been happily shoved into gardening gloves digging into soil. She kept her artist's heart, and found shared interests with talented eccentrics like the surrealist artist, Salvador Dali. And why not? She could have a connection with people in spite of her glacial, perfect countenance. She even knew how to manage the notoriously difficult Alfred Hitchcock. She was also not averse to spending time with common folk, and continued to make time for fans. According to a close confidant of the Princess, one particularly devoted supporter would be in the royal's audience once a year, swapping stories over tea.

These were the little things behind the imposing image of the ice queen. At the end of the day, she was a hometown girl who did good in Philadelphia, and who did her best to please her parents. She tried to maximize her talents wherever she found herself – on the stage, on the small screen, on the silver screen, in the role of a Princess, wife, and mother. She was open with love and affection, and she was fearless in the pursuit of what she wanted and felt she deserved. She had accomplished so much in the short time she inhabited all her incarnations.

Perhaps it is a reminder that life is not about length, but about the meaning you put into it. That it's not about the years, but about the passions you pursue, the love you seek and give, the light you shed, the art you share, the inspiration you ignite. Because if life were measured by these things, Grace Kelly continues to live on, and will outlive many of us.

Made in the USA
Lexington, KY
28 November 2019

57817730R00117